For Mike Levine

"Mike Levine was a wonderful human being, with extraordinary compassion for his readers, his editors and reporters, and the communities his newspaper served. He was a man of rare integrity, honesty and good humor.

"He was also a great community newspaper editor who used his intuitive understanding of other people's struggles with the difficulties of life to help his readers cope with and understand the complexities of the world's problems. His columns were full of human kindness.

"I know from my 50 years in newspaper publishing that Mike Levine was one of the best and most respected community newspaper editors in America."

—Jim Ottaway Jr., retired chairman of Ottaway Newspapers Inc. and former *Times Herald-Record* reporter

"One of the joys of knowing Mike were his unexpected email messages. I'd be thinking of something and he'd be thinking the same thing. He saw the world as a storehouse of important story ideas. He could see and feel those ideas. I could see that the Record was a place where the best work is encouraged and recognized and rewarded. And that was a reflection of Mike."

— Roy Peter Clark, senior scholar and vice president of the Poynter Institute for Media Studies

"Mike was the ultimate newspaper guy, from his looks to his speech to his unwavering ambition to stick up for the little guy. Every newspaper should be so lucky to have a Mike Levine writing and editing for it. His passion for newspapers and the good that could come out of them was unmatched."

— Jeff Cohen, former editor of the *Houston Chronicle* and former editor of the *Albany Times Union*

"When you first met Mike, you thought of a feisty boxer. You expected him to stand up for what he believed in. He brought with him an enthusiasm and love for our business and he loved great writing. He didn't think the size of a newspaper kept you from good watchdog journalism. And good people gravitated toward him because he was genuine."

— Gregory Favre, former president of the American Society of Newspaper Editors, former vice president of McClatchy Company and former editor of the *Sacramento Bee*

"For me, his contribution to the craft was his unrelenting cheering of people like me who see things differently, who move a little faster and who can let their batteries run down. He would jump-start us. He was the kind of guy who was always there for you. Man, the guy was so vital. He seemed like the kind of guy who was in the right place to help people. And he did."

— Ellen Foley, former editor of the *Wisconsin Journal*

More Journalism

From The Sager Group

The Stories We Tell: Classic True Tales by America's Greatest Women Journalists

New Stories We Tell: True Tales by America's Next Generation of Great Women Journalists

Newswomen: Twenty-five Years of Front Page Journalism

Next Wave: America's New Generation of Great Literary Journalists

Artful Journalism: Essays in the Craft and Magic of True Storytelling

Everybody Leaves Behind a Name: True Stories by Michael Brick

Artifex Te Adiuva

WORDS
to Repair
the
World

Stories of Life, Humor and Everyday Miracles

Cover Designed by Siori Kitajima, SF AppWorks LLC
Photo and columns, which first appeared in the *Times Herald-Record*, are
reprinted with permission.
For more information, please see www.MikeLevineBook.com

Cataloging-in-Publication data for this book is available from the Library of
Congress
ISBN-13: 978-1-950154-01-2
ISBN-10: 1-950154-01-7

Published by The Sager Group LLC
www.TheSagerGroup.net
info@TheSagerGroup.net

WORDS
to Repair
the
World

Stories of Life, Humor and Everyday Miracles

By Mike Levine

Edited by Christopher Mele

THE SAGER GROUP

Artifex Te Adiuva

For Mike's sons, Ben and Sam Levine, and Mike's wife, Ellen Levine.
May we all move closer to repair of the world through diligent listening and
painstaking care in our choice of words.

In Memory of Mike Levine
1952-2007

Acknowledgments

The road to the publication of this book was paved by a number of people whose work was instrumental.

My deep gratitude to Shaniquah Gabino, Erik Gliedman and Patti Racine at the *Times Herald-Record*, who pulled together Mike's columns from 23 years into one website. It was a Herculean task that made this book possible. Though it took me more than three years to go through all of Mike's columns, it would have taken me so much longer if not for their dedicated efforts.

Thanks to Bill Kennedy, a onetime executive editor of the *Times Herald-Record* who recognized Mike's talents and nurtured and protected him as a columnist, and to Joe Vanderhoof, the newspaper's current publisher, for permission to publish Mike's columns in this book.

My gratitude to Steve Israel, a former reporter and columnist at the *Times Herald-Record*, who cheered me on during this project. My most profound thanks to the organizers of the Mike Levine Journalism Education Fund: Taryn Clark, Barbara Gref, Ellen Levine and Meg McGuire.

Taryn was Mike's assistant, a title that hardly conveys the ways she made sure he was fed and cared for, and Barbara, a former editor at the *Times Herald-Record*, is an engine of enthusiasm who gets things done.

Ellen, Mike's widow, and Meg, Mike's former managing editor and my wife, provided the emotional support and encouragement to see this project through to its completion. They propped me up when I felt overwhelmed.

This book is a testament to the love and affection we all shared for Mike and to the enduring legacy he leaves.

Proceeds from the sales of this book will benefit the Mike Levine Journalism Education Fund to promote the kind of in-depth community news reporting that Mike so faithfully practiced for more than 20 years.

To learn more, go to www.mikelevinebook.com

Foreword

Three days a week for more than 20 years, Mike Levine wrote columns that stood up for the little guy, celebrated the lives of everyday people and shined a light on the darkness of corrupt and inept public servants.

This book represents a distillation of some of the best of those columns.

Many of you knew Mike as a columnist for the *Times Herald-Record* in Middletown, N.Y., and later as executive editor of the newspaper.

To readers he was "Mike Levine." To his colleagues he was "Mike." And to the politicians he pissed off, he was "Levine."

In life, Mike was a short guy, but in the world of journalism, he was a giant.

His columns were filled with stories of parenthood and family and of living in the Hudson Valley. He wrote about his work as an editor and columnist and served as a watchdog that challenged the arrogance of the powerful and held them accountable.

Befitting his upbringing in an Irish neighborhood in upper Manhattan and his years reporting in Sullivan County in the Catskills, he had the story-telling patter of an Irishman and a Borscht Belt sense of humor. ("The food was terrible! And the portions so small!")

Sometimes his columns veered into the schmaltzy, reaching a little too far to tug at the heart strings, and at other times he could be a little too preachy, bordering on idealism.

I say that with authority (and love and respect) after having read all 2,219 of the columns he wrote from 1983 to 2006 in preparation for this book.

Seldom, however, did Mike's columns fail to provoke a reaction, whether it was tears, laughter or anger. In some cases, his columns moved bureaucracies to right a wrong or caused elected officials to act on an issue.

He was a fierce advocate for watchdog reporting, which he believed was one of the highest callings of a newspaper.

Why was it so vital? He once said:

"Because government doesn't want us to. Because the people do.

"Because on some days, when we read yet another obituary of newspapers, watchdog reporting is all that saves us from the sin of despair.

"And, finally, because watchdog reporting is an act of faith."

Mostly, though, Mike's columns were symphonies of pacing and rhythm.

Working elbow-to-elbow with Mike on a line-edit or collaborating with him in writing was a chance to learn from a master wordsmith.

He was equal parts preacher, mentor, comic and salesman.

One of his common refrains was that articles "could not read like homework." In other words, they could not be boring. Find the tension or revealing details that would hold the reader's interest, he exhorted.

Mike believed in writing with passion and conviction, and that it was a disciplined craft, the heart of which was editing, revision and clarity.

He was an award-winning, nationally recognized writer who had chances to work in the big leagues and yet he dedicated his professional life to a scrappy tabloid whose mission was community news.

Mike did leave the *Times Herald-Record* for about a year to work at ESPN magazine in New York City for "big bucks" and to "hang out with celebs," he wrote in an Aug. 25, 2002, column.

"The new job was very cool. I worked on a well-stocked staff of talented writers and editors. We put out a slick magazine to millions every two weeks," he wrote. "The magazine was rich with unhurried wit and confident professionalism. Hot damn, start spreading the news, I had made it big in my hometown."

So why did he return to a smaller news organization with a lower profile and for less pay?

He felt a tug back to community news, he said, noting, "Maybe the tug is God's laughter as we try to avoid our mission."

But go back he did, leading and teaching a newsroom to fight above its weight class.

Working with Mike was not always easy.

When reporters chafed at the tedious work involved in getting a story, he would ask, "How bad do you want it?"

He was drawn to perfection and what felt like endless tinkering, whether it be a word choice in a story or a headline. (Sometimes I'd pitch a headline idea and he'd say: "I like the way it sounds. But I don't know what it means.")

He demanded that reporters and editors find stories in the beating hearts of their communities: What was foremost on the minds of everyday residents? He railed against coverage based on the agendas of powerbrokers and politicians.

He was aware of his demanding nature to reach for higher and better. He kept a notebook of reflections that was discovered in his car after he died.

Among the entries, he wrote:

"I have a stubborn stamina and the joke about me at work is that I'm relentless. Not a prick, not a micromanager, not personally critical, just staying there all night to play with the words one more time. I know I can be exhausting. If you come to my funeral, tell 'em I'm sorry."

Mike believed better stories were to be found in conversations with cab drivers, diner waitresses and local barbers than with mayors or council members.

And when staff members would roll their eyes at his zeal, Mike would sometimes quote an editor he once worked for: "It's not easy being good."

That was true, but Mike made it look easy. His mind was a creative hive of words.

Terry Egan, a friend and fellow editor, said: "Working with Mike was like sitting at the keyboard with Beethoven. Only there would be chicken wings all over the room and grease on the keyboard."

I recall being in Mike's office in the company of senior editors. He sat in the rolling chair at his desk, one leg tucked under his body. He had his back to us and was reading a story on the computer.

He pushed away from his desk, spun around his chair, took off his glasses, held them in his lap, folded down one of the arms and on the spot offered the perfect headline for the story.

"Wow!" I marveled to the other editors. "That's amazing. Did you see how he did that?!"

Without missing a beat, Mike quipped, "That's part of the savant of my idiot savant."

Savant or no, Mike was certainly exceptional. Yet as much as readers and some in the newsroom put him on a pedestal, he was as human as the rest of us.

He embraced that humanity, telling stories of his flaws in his columns. Sometimes they were humorous tales of what a slob he was with his car, or more serious confessions in which he held himself accountable for the shortcomings in his work.

Privately, Mike sometimes talked about the concept of "Tikkun olam." It's Hebrew for "repair of the world," and it speaks to an aspiration to behave and act constructively and beneficially for the rest of the world.

To me, he embraced that principle in his work.

Mike died in 2007 at the age of 54.

He left this world too soon, but the legacy he left behind lives on in the hearts of many. This book is a tribute to that legacy.

Thanks for everything, Mike.

Christopher Mele

Table of Contents

Acknowledgments xi

Foreword xiii

Chapter 1: Stories of How We Live 1

Some Chances Drift in the Wind 3

The Road Will Not End in Darkness 6

Different Paths in Search of Hope, Faith 10

'Family' Reunited After Twenty Years 13

Two Smooth People in a Callous World 17

Before Long, We Also Will Grow Old 20

Far Away, to Life Without Dad 23

Missing the Happiness Money Can't Buy 26

Finding the Miraculous in the Everyday World 29

Turning Up the Flame on Poverty 32

A Company Man From First to Last 35

Do Not Go Gently Into That Good Night 38

Knocking Down Walls That Separate Neighbors 41

Bureaucracy: Where Heroes Are Underdogs 44

Let Us Pause This Day, to Remember 47

In Darkest Hour, Miracles Keep Happening 49

Chapter 2: Humorous Columns 53

Slob Stories 55

Real Men Aren't Afraid of Cramps 59

It's Just a Dog...It's Just a Dog...Really 62

You Know, It's Akin to Washing Your Car 65

...And Lo, a Voice Spoke, and It Was Good: Shamefaced
Deadcrops, Arise, Fertilize 68

Better Not Mess Around With This Revolution 71

Oh Rats, Mickey Mouse 74

Oh Well, There Goes the Neighborhood   77

Lines From Diary of a Mad Homeowner   80

See the Cookie Crumble   83

The Party's Shaping Up   86

Six Months and Still Going Smokeless   89

For the Lovelorn, Some Stock Advice   92

Chapter 3: On Being a Columnist and Editor   95

Welcome Home to Your Paper   97

Nine Years Has Caused Real Change   99

City Boy Sees Country, Likes It and Stays   102

What I Learned From You   105

Chapter 4: Mike as Watchdog   107

Tangled Web Only the State Can Perceive   109

Newburgh Election Just Like Mississippi 1965   112

This Padding We Don't Need   115

Make Them Write Clearly   118

Discounting the Premium on Pretty   121

More Phony Baloney From a Meat Market   124

This Flick Rates Just One Garbage Can   127

Leaks May Hurt Politicians, But They Help Us   130

Rebel Doctor Puts Others' Health Above His Own Gain   133

Normal Isn't Always Nice   135

The Skunk Meets His Match, Odor-Wise   138

Too Young to Qualify for Justice   141

No Happy Returns on 'Psycho Selloff'   144

Chapter 5: Parenthood   147

One in a Series of Firsts   149

Precious Days   151

A Tortured Father Holds Out Hope for Lost Son   154

From Fatherhood to Misunderstood   157

In Her Eyes, You'll Always Be the Best   160

The Kids Are Going to Be Okay...Really   163

One Small Link to the Saner Side of Life   166

Mother's Bond: Gift Hallmark Can't Top   169

Chapter 6: Life in the Hudson Valley   171

You Can't Beat This Market's Selection   173

Mid-Hudson Should Hop on the Secession Bandwagon   176

Answers to Tourists' Most Pressing Questions   179

Hail, Fallonia, You're Full of Baloneya   182

A Sullivan Twist of 'Irish' Camaraderie   185

When the Doctor Was Part of the Cure   188

Area's Heritage Being Put Out to Pasture   191

Tourist Quiz Was Real Trip   194

Condoman Grips Bucolic Burg by Wallet   197

Woodstock Era: Same Stuff, Different Decade   200

Disaster Realizes Every Mother's Nightmare   203

Chapter 7: Grace, Gratitude and Connections Greater Than Ourselves   207

Searching for Visions in Our Souls, Pocketbooks   209

The Lights of Christmas Present   211

Taking a Chance on Happiness   213

Deep Down, Snow Is Child's Play   216

Making Money vs. Making Your Mark   218

It Takes a Big Heart to Hear Cry of Despair   220

Jake's October Run Still Rises in the Dust   223

Adam Finds the Light   225

A Sacred, Special Morning   230

A Little Girl's Grace Lives on at Thanksgiving   232

Find the Possibility in 2007's New Days   235

Afterword   237

About the Author   241

About the Editor   243

About Team Mike   243

About the Publisher   245

Chapter 1:

Stories of How We Live

"Telling people's stories was a way of finding out about my own. It was one of the few ways I could feel some transcendent force of life some people call God."

— Mike Levine

Some Chances Drift in the Wind

Now, dear reader, let us talk of currents in the air that cannot be explained. Of messages received and opportunities floating by, waiting, wishing to be plucked. Listen:

The air was dead when she let go. Tosha Michael watched her blue balloon dawdle above the hardscrabble fields of northern Alabama. Just when it looked like it would hover hopelessly above the treetops, a sudden wind rushed by.

The 11-year-old girl who had never seen beyond the fields watched her balloon disappear.

Bartender Bob Schlag was running late for his Saturday shift. He crossed his front yard, head down. He was almost to his car when a fresh wind rustled the oak branches, sending shadows swaying.

Schlag looked up. He saw a blue balloon dangling from a tall oak.

We know it belongs to Tosha, the shy Baptist girl from little Lexington, Alabama, whose balloon traveled 900 miles in less than a day to settle in a bartender's tree.

Schlag stared at the hanging balloon and set off to work in Glen Spey. He settled in the bartender's familiar domain of wet quarters and soggy dollar bills. He pumped beer, poured whiskey and began to wonder if that blue balloon was like a message in a bottle.

First thing next morning, Schlag looked up at the oak. The blue balloon was still hanging. He took out his rifle and, careful not to hit the balloon, shot down the branch.

It came tumbling with the balloon. A message was tied to the balloon in a plastic baggie. It said, "Dear You ... Get high on life."

On the other side of the card was Tosha Michael's address. Schlag went inside and called. He heard a young and soft southern voice:

"Yes, sir." And, "Thank you, sir." And, "Here's my mother, sir."

Then a cordial, but wary mother, "I hope you know Tosha is a fine Christian girl."

Certainly, said Schlag. We'll talk again. Bye now.

Well, dear reader, here's where this small story could end. Schlag wouldn't let it. He saw a chance to connect with folks he never would have met.

He sent a letter along with a video of Pond Eddy, the local Ukrainian festival, Hawks Nest. She sent a letter back describing her life in Alabama. They talked on the phone, she called him Uncle Bob and the whole family became friends.

A year or so later, he journeyed to Alabama.

Tosha lived in a small house stuffed with loving family. Bob and the brood hit it off great. She took him to school and showed off her new "uncle," the bartender from up north.

Schlag married five years ago to a woman with family in Tennessee. They decided to wed down there so he could invite some special guests. The marriage was witnessed by Tosha and her family.

Families intertwined. Birthdays were remembered. Tosha finished high school, waitressed and married.

Their daughter was born severely retarded. The doctors said Katelyn would die. Tosha has been with the baby operation after operation and when she gets weary, Uncle Bob bucks her up.

"Tosha looks forward to your phone calls so much," said her mom. "It makes her day."

Schlag and his wife also go down to visit. He marvels at the way Tosha carries her burdens and blesses the day he found the balloon. "It's like being honored with a whole new family," he said. "And another generation."

Bob Schlag, now a few moons from 60, was walking in the deep woods of western Sullivan. Maybe it was the way the breeze was blowing the other day, maybe it was the 10 years that had passed, but he was thinking about the balloon. What if he had just passed it by?

"Life would have been less," he told himself.

He called here with an urgent message.

Please, said Schlag, tell people to keep their eyes and ears open. We all have opportunities to connect, however briefly. It could be the person at the next seat in the diner, the passenger on the bus, any chance encounter that brings strangers together.

"We hesitate to let life in and then it is gone."

And so, dear reader, this is Bob and Tosha's story. Like the balloon that floated from Alabama, its message dangles before our eyes, waiting to be plucked before the next sudden wind sweeps it away.

The Road Will Not End in Darkness

All day long, a hazy sun heaves and locusts hum. Fish splash near weeping willows. The sky hangs still and white.

Charcoal clouds charge from the west, sending thick gray gusts rippling lakes and whipping willows. The sky goes black and boys with fishing poles scamper. Lightning crackles and thunder booms.

Heavens open.

Rob Finlay leaves work in Monroe and sets out for home and supper with Kate. God, he can hardly wait. What's a little rain when you're waiting to put your arms around Katie.

The downpour is flying past when he turns right along Walton Lake onto Laroe Road, a snaky country lane that is everyone's shortcut to Warwick. A quarter mile on the right, down the hill, he sees tail lights off the puddled road.

What's this, somebody broken down?

Rob can keep going, be home before Kate. Start supper. Turn on the music.

He remembers when he might have flown past in a daze, his faded gold '82 Caddy splashing the stranded car. He used to dwell on himself. Absorbed with his depression, his disappointment at not amounting to more than a home health aide, his private murk of self-pity.

If he went out, it was with whoever, whatever. He could feel alone with or without company. One night last year, his sister's girlfriend, Katie, was over to his parents' house.

Katie had been over before, but Rob was too taken with his misery to notice much. This night, he and Katie got to talking. She danced as she laughed, a bright summer's day of a girl, gentle as a waking breeze.

The way she listened. The peace in her story. They talked long into the night like old friends.

She said, "Hey, I could get used to you," and Rob was touched. Winds of love began to rise. His depression was a cloud that had moved on, a storm that had passed.

They talked again. Walked the wintry roads of Warwick. And on and on they opened their hearts so that Rob woke up to life and he understood something holy.

Katie was always with life. One of nine Murphy kids from Chester, she was born premature with an overgrowth of blood vessels that hung from her face. Because she was too young, the doctors could not operate.

Her parents gave her extra love for what the world might give back to her in cruelty. She woke up happy and sang like a bluebird. She was never absorbed with disfigurement.

When Katie was 12, her parents finally found a doctor who agreed to the delicate operation. The nerves in her face could easily be damaged. Three years and painful surgeries later, the birth mark was gone.

Katie blossomed as a beauty with the compassion of one who has known hurt.

What Rob saw was a walking miracle. At 18, she bounced with the energy of the truly alive. She listened so closely when others talked, they walked away feeling transformed, their troubles somehow diminished.

Katie was in this moment, this life. Her friends saw her gift. Her family cherished it.

And Rob, feeling lucky as a Lotto winner, got to be her guy. Katie was crazy for him. At the Warwick spring high school play of '97, she sang "Today I Met the Boy I'm Gonna Marry" and she winked at Rob.

So it would be Katie Murphy, Rob thought, Katie forever.

What becomes of love. Rob grew into manhood, learning to say we instead of I. He helped her through school. He helped her save up for a little used Toyota.

This spring, he searched half of Orange County for just the right wayward kitten Katie had always dreamed of owning. Oh, to be on an errand of the heart. He found Darryl and on May 3, her 19th birthday, Katie squealed with delight at their shared young one.

Rob encountered his home health care clients as people. Discovered the gifts in the most disabled of them. He listened closer.

Sometimes Katie would drop over and give his clients a big hug. Then she bounded off to the next of three jobs. Baby-sitting at 6 a.m., Orange County Community College all day, bussing restaurant tables all evening.

In June, she found a job at Camp Monroe. They loved Katie immediately and had her run the office. And a letter dated June 29, 1998, was in the mail saying Katie had made the dean's list at OCCC.

This would be a wonderful night. She'd walk in from work, he'd plant a sweet kiss on her mouth and dinner would be cooking. Music on the radio, Darryl the cat on their laps, and the lazy swoon of a summer evening.

But first, he slows down behind the tail lights off the side of Laroe Road. Two other cars have just parked behind the car. An accident. The road was always lousy with accidents.

Rob walks ahead to help. He sees a gray Toyota Tercel wrapped against a tree. Can't be.

He runs to the car. He finds Katie, sitting in the front seat with her seat belt strapped, her mouth in the shape of a smile. Her eyes are closed.

Rob leans in and shouts into her ear, "I love you, baby. You're gonna make it, baby. Everything's going to be all right."

An arriving volunteer asks Rob to step aside so he can give CPR. Please move your car farther down so the ambulance can get closer. Rob parks a quarter mile down the hill and begins running up toward Katie.

Of course, Katie's going to be OK. There's no blood. Just a bad knock made her lose consciousness for a short while.

The last 20 yards, he cannot move. He begins to pray. How is she? he asks. I need to know what to pray for.

Rob feels a cop's soft hand on his shoulder. He sees the volunteer who was giving CPR, now sitting on a car bumper, head in his hands. The man is crying.

They carry Katie out on a stretcher. The ambulance drives away. She is gone.

The next day, dazed and driven, Rob stops at the tree of death.

A sweet sun sparkles in a blue heaven. Rob has never seen a sun so yellow or a sky so blue. He feels a breeze gentle as a lover's breath.

What becomes of the storm, so sudden upon us, so quickly passed? What becomes of the fleeting sun, the burden descending, the shadow hanging from a child's face, the rip of separation, the unbearable visit of grief? One night the pain is so bad, Rob lies on the floor, writhing.

Other nights, Rob Finlay hears Katie Murphy say she is all right and with him. Alone in bed, he feels her face on his chest, her body in the shelter of his arms. Rob goes to work and the kindness she awoke in him embraces the people in his care.

What becomes of love is never ending.

Different Paths in Search of Hope, Faith

April 19, 1987

Each year, we recite the stories of Easter and Passover. Like the springtime that hosts these holidays, the stories are meant to renew us, reminding us of the roots of our faith.

In this column, the Easter-Passover season is also a time for telling the small story of two men from Newburgh — Thomas Fenlon and Hirshel Jaffe.

***

At first glance, which is all the time most of us give before we judge each other, no two men are as different as Father Thomas Fenlon and Rabbi Hirshel Jaffe.

Rabbi Jaffe is a dictionary definition of an extrovert. He's the guy at the party making introductions, backslapping strangers, telling long, impassioned stories. In his earlier rabbinical days in Dallas, he once wrestled with an attacking neo-Nazi during a demonstration. While visiting the Iranian hostages in 1980, Jaffe flaunted his free spirit in front of the ayatollah's armed guards by happily jogging around the courtyard.

Father Fenlon describes himself as "quiet and reserved." He speaks softly, choosing his words carefully. A product of an upper-middle class Westchester family, Father Fenlon humbly serves the poor Hispanic Catholics of Newburgh. Sorrow and injustice weigh heavily on him and a pessimism over the human condition is tempered only by his deep faith. "I am not optimistic," he says of the world's problems. "But I am hopeful."

Fenlon and Jaffe met nearly 15 years ago, joining forces to battle a former Newburgh school official they believed was polarizing the community. Despite their obvious differences, they felt right at home with each other.

They would jog together and the rabbi would invite the priest to his home for dinner. The two believed they enjoyed the same mission in life. Along with the Rev. Glen Henrickson, they hosted a weekly radio show.

In July of 1982, Hirshel Jaffe was felled by leukemia. One Friday night that fall, he was unable to conduct Sabbath services. Father Fenlon stepped in and spoke to the rabbi's congregation.

He prayed for his friend and recalled the biblical story of Jonathan and David. The story tells of a friendship that endured even through times of impending doom.

"The soul of Jonathan was knit to the soul of David, and Jonathan loved him as his own soul. 'Go in peace,' said Jonathan to David. 'The Lord shall be between me and you, and between my descendants and your descendants, forever.'"

Hard years passed. In the fall of 1984, Hirshel Jaffe's leukemia was complicated by a rare form of tuberculosis. It almost killed him. It also changed his way of looking at life. The rabbi fell in love with it.

Father Fenlon continued his fight for human dignity. He traveled to Central America on a mission of peace and was briefly kidnapped by Nicaraguan contras.

In the winter of 1984, the rabbi volunteered for a new, potentially dangerous treatment for leukemia. It worked. He began to recover his strength.

Jaffe the storyteller wrote a book about his illness called "Why Me? Why Anyone?" The paperback edition has just been released. He performs volunteer work with cancer patients throughout the area. Last month, he even began to jog again.

Father Fenlon continues his work with the poorest of Newburgh's poor. This past year, his friends commemorated his silver anniversary as a priest in a celebration he called, "the happiest day of my life."

Hirshel Jaffe was there. He turned to his friend, Tom Fenlon, and said, "I now pray for you as your prayed for me." The two men embraced.

In Hebrew, the rabbi recited a blessing for the priest.

***

Easter and Passover is a season when Christianity and Judaism cross paths.

We can divide ourselves by our differences and treat existence as a narrow exercise in petty prejudice.

Or we can join together in the enduring psalms that link us all — struggle and hope, love and loss, dignity and faith.

What choices our stories call upon us to make.

'Family' Reunited After Twenty Years

July 3, 1989

"And you still don't know nothing," hoots Harrison Jones of Magnolia, Ark.

Justino talks about that day by the river. May 1, 1969. He was 19 years old. The boys from Lima were crossing a river. Snipers shot at them. Justino's leg got caught in the tank tread. He fell into the river.

"See that big fat guy over there named Tex?" says Justino, lightly. He points to a man in T-shirt and sweats, working on a cigar butt and a beer. "He tried to pull me out of the river. Another Amtrack (amphibious vehicle) pulled me in. The medic said, 'You're in trouble. You lost the front of your foot.'"

All but three of the men from Lima Company 3-1 came home dead or injured. A recent letter of commendation from the Marine commandant says so.

Sunday is the first time the survivors have been together since their Vietnam combat 20 years ago. "We're closer than family," says Jones. "It's like we've never been apart."

Bobby Moulaison is the last to show. The men go over to him. "Cheez," says one. "Look at the size of his arms."

Bobby Moulaison has no legs. They were blown off by a mine. In one of his muscular arms is a photo album from Vietnam.

Now they all are here, the 10 known survivors of Lima Company 3-1. They eat. They drink beer. They break into knots of two and three and talk.

The most soft-spoken were John Jackson and Tom Kerrigan. They were lieutenants, leaders of the second and third platoons.

Their platoon's job was search and destroy along the Danang barrier. They were at the front of the front line. "These weren't the guys who got to go to the USO shows," says Kerrigan.

Kerrigan and Jackson figure more than a third of the soldiers who fought for them are dead. When one got killed or injured, another went in his place. "Just boys, we all were," Kerrigan says.

Kerrigan says he was worried about coming to the reunion. "I had to make decisions that got some of these guys hurt."

Jackson remembers the dead coming in. How it never seemed to end. How he shuddered that he might be responsible. The nights of rock 'n' roll radio in the jungle and the warm beers he found for his troops to keep up their morale. In the end, he remembers the only thing that held these boys together was each other's bravery. And how they conquered the fear in their young hearts.

One day, he had to talk a kid into fighting. "I told him to stick close to me." That was the day John Jackson got his legs mangled by a mine.

Even today, the scars overwhelm both legs. But in this crowd, Jackson doesn't have to feel self-conscious about wearing shorts.

The day grows hot. Some of the guys help Justino roast a pig. They drink beer. They tell some bawdy stories and then, in turns, grow quiet. They kid each other less as the day goes on.

Bobby Moulaison sits in the sun with his wife. He shows pictures. He says what all of them say today, that he thought about these guys all the time, wondering what had happened. He was afraid to call. "I was afraid to hear some mother say her son was dead."

Moulaison was a tunnel rat. He crawled into enemy holes not knowing if they would blow up on him. He explains it the same way most of them do. "I was just a kid," he says. "It seemed like an adventure. There was no politics to it at all."

His brain almost boiled from a jungle fever. His legs were shot off. He inhaled the smell of burning flesh and gunpowder and he never forgot it.

"We saw the South Vietnamese Army didn't want to fight," he says. "After a while, it was the hell with them, the hell with everything. We said let's do it for the (Vietnamese) kids. It's hard for people to understand, but we wanted to leave it a better place."

And he says if he had to do it all over again, he would.

That's what all the men say. It was their most intimate, intense experience. For some, it has made the rest of their lives hard. They all lead productive work lives, but some say they have been treated for depression, others for recurring nightmares. Some had failed marriages, some say they drink a little too much.

"Talk to our wives," one says softly. "See what it's like to be with us."

Some things couldn't be talked about for 20 years. They kept it inside. They had to see each other to tell of it.

Harrison Jones made it happen. Six days before Christmas, Jones from Arkansas started calling information for New York area codes and found Justino in Newburgh. Justino drove down to Arkansas and they rode 600 miles to see Tex Carruth. They all needed to talk, they agreed. They vowed to meet Independence Day weekend in Newburgh, Frank's 40th birthday.

It is now close to 3 p.m. The sun burns hotter. Holiday firecrackers explode. The men try not to flinch.

They're almost ready to eat the roasted pig, but first they pose for a group shot. They gather in the front yard next to the sign.

They smile stiffly. Bobby Moulaison takes off his artificial leg and grinning, waves it at the camera.

After the picture, they go to the backyard.

Harrison Jones begins to weep. They go to comfort him. Another man starts to break down.

"Let it go," they say to each other. "Let it out."

The men embrace.

* * *

This summer, the mass media is hyping the 20th anniversary of the Woodstock Festival. It is supposed to be a big deal because a bunch of kids listened to rock music in the rain.

In a jungle half a world away, other kids also listened to Jimi Hendrix in the rain.

They were shot and mined and tortured. They came back mangled and dead and ignored.

There will be no Life cover stories on the 20th reunion of the 2nd and 3rd platoons of Lima Company 3-1. Twenty years later, our national leaders no longer even try to articulate the reasons these boys were there.

But, yesterday, in a Newburgh back yard, 10 survivors tried to exorcise a season that may never pass.

Two Smooth People in a Callous World

The last weeks of winter blur in a mist of cold rain and fog. But for Ernest Tanous of Kiamesha Lake, not one moment of his 74 years stands any clearer than the chilly, cloudy morning of Feb. 24.

The day before, he had driven from Sullivan County to his daughter's home in Fair Oaks. It was a wonderful Sunday visit — Mary and Billy and the grandchildren were all in good spirits.

Their house was just 10 minutes away from Horton Hospital in Middletown where Ernest was scheduled to have a heart scan the next day. He decided to stay over.

He woke up the next morning feeling great. But when he hit the cold air to get into his 1980 Chevy, Ernest began to feel a little off. Well, he was on this way to the hospital, anyway, he figured. Maybe he just had too much to eat the day before. Everything would be all right.

The drive to Middletown was difficult. He continued to feel worse. Pains in his chest. Short of breath.

Something was wrong.

He parked the Chevy on hilly Ridge Street, a block away from the hospital. He opened the car door. It was all getting very confusing.

He started to walk in the street toward the hospital. With each step up the hill, he searched for air. He found only pain.

About 10 yards from his car, Ernest Tanous crumpled onto the pavement. He knew he must get up. He tried. He saw a car coming down the street. Help at last.

The car passed him by.

And another.

And another.

Ernest struggled to his feet and stumbled toward his car. The door was still open. He made it to the edge of the driver's seat.

He sat there, half in, half out of the car, dazed and sick. No one was helping. He was having a heart attack and his life was slipping away.

At that moment, a car pulled alongside 22 Ridge St. It was Mary Jenne's ride to Middletown High School. Mary, 15, opened the door to her house and saw a man across the street sitting on the edge of a car. "Help," gasped Ernest Tanous. "I need help."

Mary raced inside. "Daddy, daddy," she shouted. "Come quick. Somebody's in trouble."

Harvey Jenne, 54, was home only because he was recovering from a recent hernia operation. Sitting in the kitchen having coffee, he heard his daughter's shouts and hurried out of the house.

He saw Ernest Tanous on the edge of the driver's seat, semi-conscious. Disregarding his hernia problem, he pushed Ernest over to the passenger's side and jumped in the car. The keys were still in the ignition.

He sped up the block to the emergency room exit, ran inside and said, "I think I have a heart attack victim."

Doctors, nurses, aides were out to the car in seconds. They brought Ernest in and began work. Harvey Jenne waited in the emergency room. "It doesn't look good," he was told. They kept working.

An hour later, Ernest Tanous was resting comfortably in the coronary unit. Harvey came in to see him. "That's the man," Ernest Tanous said. "That's the man who saved my life."

***

Ernest Tanous recounts the moments he spent on the street wondering why people in cars didn't stop to help. He knows they could have been the final thoughts of his life. "I am here because of a wonderful man," he says.

For his part, Harvey Jenne doesn't want the hero treatment. "Anyone would've done the same," he says. "It was just the decent thing to do. My daughter deserves the credit. I didn't do anything special."

What's special is this:

Endless episodes of callousness — like drivers leaving a man to die on the street — seem to define the human race a cruel. But it takes only one act of decency to disprove that definition.

And, for that, we join Ernest Tanous in thanking Mary and Harvey Jenne.

Before Long, We Also Will Grow Old

Arthur Taylor went down to the city for pleasure. All he got was lost. Standing there on the crowded subway platform, in his Sunday best, he was helpless as a 27-year-old former combat soldier could ever be.

Better get directions. Was it a coincidence Arthur asked the prettiest lady on the platform?

"Ma'am, I'm down here from Newburgh, and I was wondering if you could tell me how I can get to this address."

She didn't know where Newburgh was and had only a vague idea about the address the stranger was looking for. She herself had come up from North Carolina, was working as a hospital attendant and going to night school.

They got to talking. One thing led to another and out of Arthur's mouth came a truth he could not hold inside. "You are the prettiest lady I've ever seen," he said.

Her name was Eva, and Arthur would come down to the city to take her on proper dates.

"Eve," he would say, calling her that because to him, she was the only woman in the world. "I'm saving my money so we can get married."

He'd say that every date until, one day, Eve said, "Arthur, you aren't ever going to have the money. Let's just get married."

Pick the date, honey, he said.

And she did. June 25, 1947. And they did and they were one. They walked out of old Reform Episcopal Church on Newburgh's South Street, tall with life's promise.

They worked hard. Arthur was as sturdy as the Balmville tree. Day in, day out, year after year, he toiled at Tarkett, the floor tile factory in Vails Gate.

Eve became a certified alcoholism counselor and a substitute teacher. They raised four children.

Eve got the girls involved in Brownies and Girl Scouts. Arthur would take the family to Brooklyn Dodger games and when the team left, he took them to the Mets. They went on family picnics, bright lakeside days of food and harmony.

Arthur worked at Tarkett tile for 40 years. Worked his way up to foreman. They bought a home on Grand Street.

The children grew up straight and true and moved away. The years ground away. Arthur wore down.

Six years ago, Arthur was working at Tarkett on the upper deck when he felt sick. He stumbled downstairs and lay down on a bench in a supervisor's office.

He never got up.

The stroke hit him hard. Eve took care of him as best she could. But Arthur, 72, needed a nursing home.

Because Arthur's hard-earned pension put them slightly above Medicaid limits, the nursing home said the Taylors would have to pay $500 a month.

They didn't have $500 anymore. After 40 years of work, between taxes and groceries and car insurance and just the cost of staying alive, there was nothing left.

Arthur didn't want to burden his wife. Sure didn't want to tell his kids. He lied to Eve. Sure, I can come home, he said, I don't need this place. I can get around.

The other day, Eve signed Arthur out. When he came home, it was clear he could not get around at all. Couldn't even get from his wheelchair to the toilet.

Eve tried her best but Arthur was too tall and his body was out of control. He lay helpless.

She ran out toward South Street in search of help. The same street she and Arthur had married on almost 46 years ago. Now returning as a 72-year-old woman looking for someone to help her husband onto the toilet seat.

She paid two drunks $10 to get the job done. She did the same thing the next morning. This wouldn't do.

She called the nursing home Monday. She said they told her Arthur couldn't return. Desperate and sobbing, she called someone, anyone for help. It happened to be me.

"This is a good man," she said. "This shouldn't be happening to him."

It shouldn't be happening to either of them. These are people who played by the rules their whole lives. Raised a family, contributed to their community. This is a man who worked until he dropped.

I told Mrs. Taylor I'd be over and gave her the number to the county hotline. By the time I got to her place, a county official was already there. Calls were made.

I don't know if it was the fear of bad press or the chance to do the right thing, but the nursing home suddenly said Arthur's bed was waiting for him. The county will help out for a short time through an emergency fund.

There are millions of Taylors out there. Most don't get rescued. They are buried in bedrooms, in need of a hand.

Before spring is out, a national health plan will be hatched. It will cost money. It will raise taxes.

We may whine about the burden. We may vote it down.

The Taylors' story is told here because they are us. Their lives are ours.

Someday we, too, will be old and we will beg for dignity.

Far Away, to Life Without Dad

October 6, 1991

Boxes fill the house. One by one, they will be sealed and marked, to be loaded onto a rented van. The family will drive the van across the rolling hills of Pennsylvania, far, far away to a big farm.

But now it is bedtime in the Eppenbach house in Greenville. What do you want to talk about, the mother asks her children?

"We will talk about Daddy," says Heidi, who is about to be 3. She starts chirping, "Daddy, daddy, daddy, daddy."

"Don't," says her 4-year-old brother, Horst. "It will make you get sick and spit up."

The mother swallows hard.

Heidi knows her father only through things packed away in boxes — through pictures and stories and the wedding rocking chair and the clock he built that still ticks. Mostly, she must construct a father out of other people's memories.

The last time she felt his embrace, she was 12 weeks old. That was the day her father was murdered.

The boy was 2 years old. He was in the room when the state police came in to talk to his mother.

The boy remembers everything about his father. They were inseparable. His dad could make anything, build anything. He would follow his dad around carrying a toy tool box. Daddy's little helper.

He'd listen closely as his dad told him about putting things back where he found them. They'd go everywhere together. Horst couldn't understand how men could waste their time in bars when they had children at home to love.

They would have gone together the day of the murder if little Horst wasn't in his pajamas.

These days, the boy smiles some, does his chores religiously. Most of the time he walks around like Daddy, everything under control, everything in its right place.

Then suddenly the boy pretends to shoot everything in sight. He gets so intense, he shakes. He wants Daddy to fix his broken toys.

The doctors call it a post-traumatic stress disorder.

The mother knows it's a broken heart. And she has to walk the boy through the story again.

"Daddy went to help a neighbor. When he got there, a man was being mean to her. Daddy went to help the lady and the man hurt Daddy very badly."

"God couldn't fix him?" asks the son.

"God took Daddy home," says the mother.

The mother kisses Heidi good night. She kisses young Horst. Sometimes, he acts so much like a little man. She wants him to be the little boy he is.

She leaves the bedroom to face the boxes.

This was their dream, her and Horst. They would one day move to a farm with the kids. He'd watch her sit in the rocking chair he made for their wedding. She'd watch her husband and little Horst building something outside. Heidi would be feeding the chickens.

They planted those seeds together, this dream, this life, these children.

It was a January day in 1989. The elder Horst went to check on a neighbor and walked in on the middle of a rape. Horst tried to help her. He was shot to death.

It occurs to Susan Eppenbach the killer is walking around, maybe not far away, going about his business.

Susan Eppenbach is a realist. Never for a minute does she wake up and think Horst is still alive. She is too busy keeping her family together to spend her time wishing for what she cannot have.

There is one thing she hopes for. She wants the man who

murdered her husband caught. "For what this killer did to our kids alone," she spits out.

For the daughter who still colors pictures for her dead father, pictures that must be stuffed in boxes alongside the remains of her daddy's life.

For the lost boy walking around with his tool box asking people to put things back where they found them.

State police say there is no prime suspect in the Horst Eppenbach murder, although they say the trail is "not completely cold." They still believe the killer was local.

"That's why the chances of closing it are very good," says Troop F Commander Major Ed Kelly. He can't say when. He says no one can.

This week, Susan Eppenbach will seal the boxes and load the van. The children will say goodbye to the house where Daddy held them. They will begin their drive to the faraway farm.

At that very moment, Horst Eppenbach's killer might be sleeping soundly or eating well. But he should know this.

Somewhere in the night, where fatherless children sleep, justice is calling.

Missing the Happiness Money Can't Buy

The businessman speaks in stops and starts. He searches for words and doesn't find them.

He fidgets in his swivel chair. His dark baggy eyes dart around his cramped office, from dirty coffee cups to mountains of papers to an autographed picture of a clown. They finally rest on a framed photo of a woman. He bites his lip and looks away again.

"I'm trapped," he says. "I got nowhere to turn. I got no one to talk to."

This is the story he tells a stranger.

He first met her seven years ago. He had to have her. He even dated a friend of hers to get close. He shot all the angles.

When he got his opening, he blew in with gifts of jewelry and clothes. In six weeks, they were engaged.

After they married, he started a business in Brooklyn.

He played the game smart, put in the long hours. The business took off.

He made more money than he had ever known. He bought his wife more jewelry, more clothes. "Here, take her shopping," he would say to her mother. "Make sure she buys plenty."

He and his wife did the town. They invested in real estate. They traveled in the fast lane.

They grew distant.

He remembers someone in her family saying to him, "Your wife doesn't want all those material things anymore. She wants you."

The businessman was shaken. Giving things was how he showed love. He was never good at "all that communication stuff." What could he do?

Maybe the country would be a good idea. Time to get out of the damn city and start a family.

He bought a thriving business in the mid-Hudson. They moved up here last year. They gave birth to a child seven months ago. Maybe they would find happiness.

She hated it. He spent long hours on the business. When he came home, he thought she was more distant than ever.

He didn't know how to talk about it with her. He bought her more gifts. She thanked him a million miles away.

He began to feel his wife's family was telling her what a jerk he was. He began to suspect his wife agreed.

One day, a strange woman he would never love paid attention to him. It felt good. He hated himself for it.

He says his wife accused him of having an affair and that she'd divorce him if she convinces herself that he has. He denied it. They go round and round on it with no way out.

Lately, she sounds farther away than ever. For his birthday the other day, he says his wife signed her birthday card "From, _____." He looked for the "love" but didn't find it. He wanted to say something to her. He didn't know how.

The businessman breaks off his story there. His mouth hangs in sadness. He can look at nothing but the ceiling.

"I watched my baby smile the other night," he says. "It was true love. All I had to do was smile back."

"My wife and my child are my whole world. I want to rebuild our love and I don't know how to tell her.

"I don't know why I act the way I do. I ask myself and I don't know. I've got to do something."

His hand reaches for the telephone.

"Well, thanks for listening," he tells the stranger. "What do I owe you? Nothing? Here let me write you out a check. No? A gift then.

What do you want? Let me send you something for your kid. No? What then?"

***

This is the story of another failed escape from the city. Of a man who tried to flee his problems by running to this area only to find they followed him and intensified.

Who, finding all escape routes now blocked, is trapped by his terrible pain. And for the first time wonders aloud what made the time bomb tick.

In the bowels of a crumpled office, he begins the long search for happiness. He picks up the phone and calls a babysitter.

"Yes, for tonight," he says in an urgent voice. "I'm taking my wife out. We've got to talk."

Finding the Miraculous in the Everyday World

June 20, 1990

Look around, we are told, look around and we will see the miracles.

Sixty-five years ago on Cuba's Isla de Pinos, Ernest West came into the world to join a starving family of 9.

He watched his father die. He watched his mother ride off on a horse to clean the homes of the wealthy. Ernest survived on corn meal.

Sometimes his mother would bring them an egg from the houses she cleaned. One Christmas, when the rich overflowed with kindness, Ernest was given a single grape. He looked at his hungry sister. He cut the grape in half and put it in her mouth.

On good days, he walked long miles to and from school. Then the rains would come, the river would rise and Ernest was trapped. When he turned 11, it was time to pick sugar cane for the rest of his life. Years passed and Ernest got married.

World war arrived and the teenager volunteered for the U.S. Army. He was sent to Miami to await orders. He got on a city bus and sat behind the driver. The driver told him "colored" passengers had to get to the back.

West did not understand English. He didn't move. He was thrown in jail and released into the Army.

After 18 months in the service, Ernest returned to Miami and sent for his wife. They were walking from the airport on Flagler Avenue when he was arrested again.

It was against the law for a black man to walk with a white woman. West's wife is mulatto.

He washed dishes in Miami. He came north to New York City. A switchblade to his throat on a Harlem street sent him scurrying to the Hudson Valley.

Twenty-two years ago, Ernest became the custodian at Round Hill Elementary School in Blooming Grove.

Something about the kids there touched him.

When they lost their lunch money, he would quietly slip them nickels and dimes. He couldn't stand to see a child go without milk.

Just one thing, he asked the kids, do not throw away food. Even if they did, he'd say, "I do not have it in my heart to be angry."

He kidded, he chatted, he reassured, he touched them with kindness. Once, a troubled child resisted the help of teachers. West told the kid he needed a sign painted. The child painted the sign for him. West gave him $25.

Frightened homesick first-graders hung on to his leg for dear life. Why did they always pick his leg to wet on? West joked.

Year after year, kid after kid, Ernest West was their favorite. "West the Best," they called him.

West the Best has to retire this week. The kids got together and pooled their nickels and dimes. They had a plaque made for Ernest, writing the inscription themselves. They gave it to him Friday. "To Mr. West, a friendly, helpful man." It will hang above the cafeteria garbage can, for the food the children do not waste.

The grown-ups gave West a fancy dinner in town. The kids wrote poems and letters to him. "Dear Mr. West," wrote third-grader Keith Porsch. "I hope you have a good life. I will miss you."

One young Yankees fan who long argued with Mets fan West broke down and bought the janitor a Mets mug. West bought the child a beautiful satin Yankees jacket.

Friday, his last day of work, will be the icing on the cake. Ernest West will be sworn in as a U.S. citizen. He is so proud, he is walking into the Goshen courtroom wearing a tuxedo.

He says, "I feel like I am the president."

A nice story, you say, but where is the miracle? Maybe there is none.

Of course, Ernest West could have eaten the solitary grape that was his only Christmas present. Instead, he shared it with his sister.

He could have cursed the country that threw him into jail for the color of his skin. Instead, he measured the land by its wonders.

He could have looked at comfortable kids throwing away food and been disgusted and bitter. Instead, he gave them love and pennies, each gift erasing the hardness of his childhood.

Look around, we are told, look around and we will see the miracles.

Turning Up the Flame on Poverty

Mattresses are flung on empty spaces on the floor where hungry children sleep. A baby weeps.

In the still heat, a mother sighs.

Thunder cracks the Walden twilight. She hears the fire siren and remembers the evening of June 7.

It was just before dinner. Gloria Gonzalez came out of the shower and saw light bulbs flickering. Then the TV her kids were watching fizzled. Smoke began to snake from the walls.

Suddenly, flames engulfed the attic.

The family raced to safety in the Walden streets. Dave, the 12-year-old, ran back into the house to try and save the family dog. He couldn't get past the flames.

Gloria's mouth grows still. A sweep of lightning and a blast from fire engines triggers a more distant memory.

She talks of the early days in the Bronx streets and the nights at the orphanage. And the day 14 years ago when she arrived in the mid-Hudson and blessed the country air for the hope it sparked.

She remembers the working days at the upholstery factory in Newburgh. The job at Letchworth Village. The job's end, the beginning of life on welfare, and the hope that vanished in smoke.

So Gloria Gonzalez and her five children stood outside on the afternoon of June 7 and watched themselves become homeless. When they went back in after the fire, little what they owned remained. A few clothes and a few sticks of furniture. The precious food stamp check was found soiled and unusable.

Things went downhill from there.

The day after the fire, she went to Orange County Social Services. She was given $40 and was told she would not get another nickel until she had a new address. This is like a hospital telling a sick man to come back when he feels better.

Gloria Gonzalez had nowhere to turn. She thought of finding some open land and gathering her children there to sleep.

Another Walden mother on social services took pity on the Gonzalez family. Mary Tuna, with three children of her own to feed, took in Gloria Gonzalez and her five children. She shared what little food she had.

For three weeks, the two mothers and eight children have lived on small portions from this menu:

Corn flakes.

Potatoes.

Macaroni.

Salt.

Gloria Gonzalez watches her kids and wonders if she should put them in foster homes so they can eat. She worries about her older boys, hungry and cramped in their new surroundings, roaming the streets of Walden after dark.

On Wednesday, more than three weeks after the fire, Gloria Gonzalez receives a $191 check from social services. She places a call from a laundromat pay phone.

"I have to find work, we can't go on like this," she says. "I've been thinking about the children. All I want for them is to grow up independent, to learn a trade. So life can't hurt them. They need..."

The operator comes on the line and tells the mother her time is up. "Signal when through, please."

The next word from Gloria Gonzalez is "goodbye."

***

Those who have never missed a meal may moralize about welfare. They may even kid themselves into thinking it is used mainly by people living high off the taxpayer.

But if you start off life on the wrong foot, you can spend your life hanging on a rope. A fire before dinnertime three weeks ago burned the rope Gloria Gonzalez held for her family. They fell a long way before the safety net finally caught them.

They have landed only to discover the safety net is located halfway into hell.

A Company Man From First to Last

He was born, the son of farmhands, into their life of lonesome labor. Seven years before the start of this century, they drifted around the farms of Goshen and Middletown, toiling from field to field and sun to sun.

Harry Decker's mother was a stern and sturdy woman with a soft spot for her son. She made him go to school through third grade. But then Harry was needed in the fields. No more school, no more buddies.

He grew into manhood, a big, strong six-footer, and he left the farms for the company of the city. Found a trade as a laundryman in Middletown.

World war burst. Uncle Sam Wants You signs beckoned. Harry enlisted.

The boys from Middletown and Otisville formed Company I of the first New York Infantry. It was all the camaraderie Harry ever wanted. "My buddies," he called them.

While he was at boot camp, Harry's mother saved up money for a gift for her son going off to war. She sent him a banjo. Harry couldn't play much but he was so touched, he had a picture taken with it, and sent it home to her.

The boys from Middletown fought a bloody trench war in French Verdun. Company I suffered heavy losses. But they were responsible for helping to break the famous German Hindenburg line. Many of Harry's friends died.

When peace was declared, the boys blew up an ammo dump.

Harry came back home and married. He got a job as a railroad detective. It was lonely work. Harry would spend cold nights in track brush staking out thieves.

Much of his social life revolved around "his buddies" from Company I. In 1951, he formed the Last Man's Club. They bought a magnum of champagne. The idea was that the last of the 60 men to live would drink it in memory of the others.

Harry's wife died in 1963. He was alone. At night, he'd go out and drink with the fellows. Don't bother buying me a bottle, Harry would say to friends, I don't drink at home. Just when I'm out with friends.

Death cut the numbers of the Last Man's Club. In 1977, only six survived. The youngest was 80.

Harry decided the six of them should drink the bottle of champagne. He figured he might be the last survivor. And he didn't want to drink alone.

They met at the Globe Hotel, talked about old times and sang. "Nights are long since you went away...I think about you all of the day...Your buddy misses you." It was 3 a.m., everyone had gone home and Harry sat at the bar alone. His company had left.

Last September, Harry Decker became the last man of the Last Man's Club.

He still lived alone in the house where he and his wife lived, not one stick of furniture changed since she died. He'd eat every night at the Colonial Diner. For company he'd visit the Pit Stop and Chi Chi's and maybe a couple other places where they still knew him.

Last week, at age 92, Harry Decker checked in to Horton Hospital. His kidneys were failing.

He let go of this world. First, he called a few of his drinking friends to say so long. Last Friday, he told his son-in-law, "There's a banjo up in my attic. My mother gave it to me." Nobody in his family had ever known Harry owned a banjo. It was between him and his mother.

In the evening, his daughter fed him a dish of ice cream. It was his last meal. He slipped into unconsciousness and died the next day.

All day Tuesday, surviving family and friends filed past his open casket. It was good so many people showed.

Harry Decker would have enjoyed the company.

Do Not Go Gently Into That Good Night

September 4, 1988

Tired of "mall maneuvering," Rosemarie McCaffery stands with her shades and cane outside of J.C. Penney and loudly cracks blind jokes to a friend.

"Blind woman walks into J.C. Penney's," says Rosemarie, "and she starts spinning her seeing eye dog around her head. So the manager says, 'Can I help you, ma'am?' Woman says, 'No thanks, I'm just looking.'"

At the very vision the joke suggests, Rosemarie lets go with a dark crackle of laughter.

***

She lived like a lot of us. House up here, two kids, job in Manhattan. Maybe Rosemarie McCaffery found it a little tougher than most.

The house was a rented apartment in Minisink. She was raising the kids by herself. And her job as an insurance underwriter became harder to do. She kept wiping her glasses. She kept cleaning her lenses.

She kept seeing less.

In 1980, she finally went to a doctor, who beat around the bush. He said things like "progressive myopia" and "uhum" and "ahem."

Rosemarie thought about an old John Garfield movie and decided she'd try on the part. She said to the doctor, "I'm a tough broad. Give it to me straight."

He said, "You're going blind."

She grabbed the doctor by his lapels and shook him. "You sonofabitch," she screamed. "What are ya' telling me I'm going blind?"

It took five years for the world to go dark before her eyes. She cleaned one contact lens so hard, it broke. By that time, she turned her anger inside.

She spent 20 hours a day in bed, rising just to help her teenage kids off to school. A half-hour before they came home, she'd get up and pretend she'd been busy all day. Some days she could hold a book against her eyes and make out words. Some days she wouldn't open her eyes.

In March '86, she got a cane and a mobility instructor, but she had no use for either. She scratched the cane against the floor, so the instructor would think she had been practicing.

Her mobility instructor said things couldn't get much worse. That night, she got a call that her younger brother died of cancer. Growing up, he had been her protector. When her blindness drove her to bed, he chided her, "If you're going to be blind, be good at it."

For the first time since that visit to the doctor, she cried. And she cried and she cried. She cried for her brother and she cried for her blindness.

After a week, she stopped. She told herself at least she has a chance for something. Her brother had no chance.

Rosemarie decided she didn't want to spend the rest of her life in bed collecting disability checks. She got her cane, called her mobility instructor and at 42 years old, took the first steps into her new world.

She went to Manhattan in the furnace heat and the freezing cold. On buses. Subways. Crossing busy streets. OK, 40th and Fifth. Yep, Fifth goes down and that must be the traffic going east. Or is it west? Here I go.

She enjoyed music again. She listened to her childhood heartthrob Jackie Wilson and she listened to Stravinsky. Robust, forceful music. "My kind of men," she said.

Her sister Ronnie in Unionville stuck close by. They go out and try to con people into thinking Rosemarie drove the car to the restaurant. On steamy summer afternoons, they put ice cubes in beer and tell bawdy stories.

When she tells her kids something they don't want to hear, she asks them to stop making a face. "You're not blind, mom," they scream. Rosemarie says, "Yes, I am. I'm just not dumb." The kids vow to learn sign language.

On some days, she gets blue without warning, a storm rising in her hazel eyes. This summer, a tornado swept close to her house when she was alone, sending furniture crashing. She grabbed for a chair and stuck her hand in the blade of a fan. She sat on the stairs and wept in the black night.

Rosemarie dreams in full color. She dreamed her son marries and a baby is born. She was holding the baby and the room was awash in greens and whites. "How beautiful, Georgie," she told her son. Then ink begins to spill, running through the room like it would blacken a page. She woke up.

Every morning when she awakes, there is that split second of wonder before she opens her eyes when she asks herself, "Is being blind the dream?"

In the last couple of weeks, she felt a pressure in her left eye. The last faint glimmer of light is fading.

***

It has been a tough session of mobility training. She is tired, frustrated, so she tells blind jokes in front of J.C. Penney. She takes off her glasses and howls.

Rosemarie McCaffery uses whatever it takes to feel the light. A light she can touch with her hands, a light she can feel in her gut. Anger. Memory. Stravinsky. Jackie Wilson. Her sister. Her dead brother. Her kids. And, yes, even laughter raging against the inevitable journey to black, bouncing like a hammer against the shiny store windows and soothing lights of Orange Plaza.

Rosemarie's display disturbs the shoppers who duck their heads in pity and embarrassment. How unsightly.

We turn away from the woman with the beautiful eyes, comforted in our illusion that she alone walks in darkness.

Knocking Down Walls That Separate Neighbors

I rifled through the column mail. Letter after letter with definite responses to my definite opinions. This is right. This is wrong. This is the way it should be.

You and I, we all know so much.

That's when I came across the letter postmarked from the tiny village of Jeffersonville. Written by Audrey Stienstra, the words were scribbled fast, like a message in a bottle. The tenses flew from past to present, filled with lingering doubt and urgent questions.

Audrey Stienstra wrote about her neighbor Marjorie Haas. Mrs. Haas has "lived alone since her son committed suicide and her husband passed away."

Not much is known about her, wrote Audrey Stienstra.

Some of the old-timers recollect Marjorie Haas was born in 1914. Folks in town knew she was an artist who painted beautifully. She was well-educated. She ate only natural foods and used only the bare necessities. She was considered odd.

"A few neighbors would try to show an interest in her well-being. She wanted to just be left alone!" she wrote.

"Now where do we concerned neighbors draw the line when she appears to be ailing, incoherent and possibly had a stroke? No heat, she's not able or strong enough to make a fire in her wood stove. She stays in one room with an antiquated electric heater struggling to keep her warm. In below zero temperatures.

"But she wouldn't allow us to take over. Sometimes, she wouldn't answer her phone. Lights were always turned off at dusk and not used 'til dawn. It was bitter cold.

"Marjorie wanted to be alone. Where to go, what to do to get some mandatory help? We reported her plight to state police and public health. No one knows if they did anything.

"One day, a neighbor who went to her house couldn't get a response by phone or by pounding on the doors and windows. She called the sheriff's department. My husband helped the sheriff's deputy enter the house.

"They found Marjorie Haas dead under the kitchen table.

"Maybe she wanted it that way. But where were the agencies that were supposed to help? Did we, as neighbors, miss the mark? Did we care enough?

"Here is a woman with the gift to paint. Life must have meant a lot to her. She must have suffered pain and hunger in the end and the isolation of 'all alone' and to die of 'all alone.'

"She had nobody. She stays in the Harris hospital morgue. Not even an obituary in the paper."

And so Audrey Stienstra brings us her questions.

How close do we get to people who throw a wall around themselves? Should we try to knock down the wall, assuming it is only made out of loneliness and fear? Or do we respect others' boundaries and not project our values on them?

What does it mean to be our brother's keeper? What rationalizations do we carry to their graves? What mysteries of the soul must we hold in awe?

Audrey Stienstra is aware that these questions run against our need to be certain of everything. "If I wait to find a way to copy this over," she writes in closing, "I'd probably throw it away. God bless. Sincerely, Audrey Stienstra."

I'm glad she wondered out loud about Marjorie Haas, who died alone March 1 and was buried without a service.

Some lead lives filled with exclamation points. Others leave behind questions. If we listen to those questions, say people of spirit, it can lead us to wisdom and action.

As it did for Audrey Stienstra, who struggles with the questions left behind by Marjorie Haas. And who passes them on to us. In this way, she has rescued Marjorie Haas from oblivion.

Audrey Stienstra wrote this sacred letter of obituary that survives the hard body found in the bitter cold. And whose questions linger long after our certain answers crumble to dust.

Bureaucracy: Where Heroes Are Underdogs

He was the oldest of six and he did the job well. He showed the young ones how to play. When it came time for their venture onto the mean streets, Mike took them under his wing. His mom thought of him as the little protector.

So did Bridget Clancy, the girl down the street across from P.S. 201. She was 12 years old, roller skating on the East Bronx sidewalks, when some bully boy started picking on her. Mike Auer, also 12 years old, shut him up. It was the first time she laid eyes on her hero.

Days folded into seasons; shy hellos grew into long talks and in time their teenage hearts skipped a beat at the very sight of each other. She liked the quiet boy from the city who longed for the great outdoors. She admired his sense of fairness, his sticking up for the underdog. He liked her independence, her outgoing ways, her smarts.

They were King Mike and Queen Bridget of the 1971 Aquinas High School prom. He worked as a plumber's assistant until he got his draft notice. No complaining, it was time to protect his country. But he couldn't leave Bridget hanging.

He graduated from basic training and that night at 11, in a small room in Columbia, S.C., they married. A year later, Bridget Ann was born.

Boys were fighting a war then and the Army was no career training school. Mike was a combat infantryman. When he came back from Southeast Asia, he found a job working maintenance. He and Bridget moved to Mount Vernon and then, in 1979, to Sullivan County.

God, he loved the great outdoors. He got a job working maintenance at the Homowack Lodge. They bought a modest bungalow in Bloomingburg. They had three more daughters. Bridget joined the volunteer ambulance corps.

Mike fished and hunted. He was at peace in the woods. Through his work and his hobbies, he tried to add to the fairness of the world. He brought his catch of fish to the needy elderly and packed their freezers with venison. He worked as a handyman around their homes. At the country jamborees and church parties, he'd always dance with the women who were alone.

During March of last year Mike was carrying carpets at the Homowack when he felt his chest tighten. He tried to walk it off but by the time he was brought to Ellenville Hospital, he was having a heart attack. The doctors told Bridget that Mike had suffered severe muscle damage.

Mike was down, but he figured he had paid his taxes; his family would be protected until he could get back to work.

Social Security said he had to wait six months before he could apply for disability. Worker's comp also said he had to wait six months before the premium waiver would go into effect. They needed food for the kids. SSI said no.

The medical bills kept mounting. Sometimes they had to choose between medicine or dinner. Mike changed. He became a ball of quiet fury.

Bridget worked three full-time jobs at once. She'd start at the 17M deli, then go clean houses, and then work as a nurse's aide at Arden Hill Life Care.

It tore Mike up. Bridge watched him grow bitter. When she went to campaign for his benefits, he'd tell her forget it, nobody's going to help. His Social Security disability was rejected. Worker's comp kept him hanging. Mike was too mad to talk. He would stay in the woods all day. Sometimes he came home with a fish for the family.

Finally, in February, the doctor gave him permission to ease back into work very slowly. Mike worked with a vengeance, trying to make up for lost hours, lost pay, lost pride. They were deep in the hole financially.

The bitterness festered. They tried to turn the corner. They planned a fishing trip out on Islip for Memorial Day weekend. It would be Mike's birthday.

A week ago Tuesday, Mike was planting tulips around the house when he began to feel nauseous. I'm OK, he told Bridget. She was at work that night taking care of the Alzheimer's patients when 13-year-old Bridget Ann called. Dad's not feeling well again, mom, you better come home.

Bridget raced home to her childhood hero.

The next day, Bridget was talking with two men in her living room, when she heard the telephone ring. She picked up the receiver. The voice on the other end said he was from Social Security. The administration had reversed itself, he said. Mike Auer was indeed entitled to disability benefits all along. His papers were ready.

"You're too late," said Bridget Auer. "My husband died this morning."

Let Us Pause This Day, to Remember

He was 19 years old. He wrote home at every chance. Last thing Bob Peterson told his parents was "don't worry."

A few weeks ago, we went searching for him.

The train rolled through the lowlands of Holland. Out from Amsterdam where Anne Frank once hid, from Central Station where the Nazis rounded her up and sent her on a cattle car to slaughter. Past the flat fields of cows and sheep, which made the country easy pickings for the Nazi conquest. Chugging now past the peaceful Dutch farmers whose houses they overran.

We got off at Maastricht, 14 miles from the German border. It is a small, orderly city where everyone plays a musical instrument and everyone buys flowers for their Sunday visits. We bought red carnations.

We stepped onto a bus that rumbled out of Maastricht toward the German border. At last, the flatlands gave way to rolling hills and deeper sky. A big airplane appeared moments after takeoff, leaving a trail of white smoke.

Bob Peterson always wanted to fly, ever since he was a kid. He was the kind of big-hearted boy the family revolved around and they couldn't wait for him to get home. He said he had to keep flying until the job was done.

He wrote his parents that he had met a special girl in England, name of Margaret Powers. "Sounds like a movie star," he wrote.

Sweet and pretty. After this business is over, he said earnestly, "I'll be putting all my efforts toward her."

We got off the bus just before the German border on a field with the golden colors of van Gogh. Across the road was a gate that led to deep green grass and Garden of Eden-like trees with brilliant red blossoms.

And then up over a slight hill, we saw. Rows of white marble crosses as far as the eye could see. Thousands upon thousands, acre after acre, every one of them the grave of an American boy.

They all died near the end of the war. They were killed penetrating the last lines of the Nazi defense. They gave their lives to at last put an end to this horror.

It was March 14, just months before the war ended. Navigator Bob Peterson flew between Hanover and Kassel. Shots were fired and the plane came tumbling to earth.

The Department of War wrote his parents. They said they were truly sorry and what would the parents want done with their boy's body. His parents remembered Bob once mentioned that if anything should happen, leave his body over there. They shouldn't be blue because his spirit would keep flying.

A couple from Maastricht wrote that they had adopted the care of Bob Peterson's grave. He would stay in their hearts as "their liberator." They are probably dead now, too.

We searched for his grave carrying the red carnations. Section B, Row 3, Plot 29.

Past the Christian crosses and Jewish stars and fields of young soldiers with their dates of death.

When we found the white marble cross of Robert Peterson, we placed the red carnations. He is family and we wept. What if?

Maybe he and Margaret Powers would have married and had children. Maybe he would be enjoying his golden years, playing with his grandchildren on this beautiful holiday weekend.

There are thousands of Bob Petersons in graves, in ocean bottoms, their bones petrified in rocky hillsides. Their lives unlived. Their children unborn. Their sacrifice unacknowledged.

If we pass this day without one moment of gratitude, we are unworthy of their great offering.

In Darkest Hour, Miracles Keep Happening

March 3, 1989

The mother sits at the breakfast table, eating nothing but cigarette smoke. She exhales a cloud that lingers in front of her ashen face and gray eyes. She talks about unpaid bills that are as thick as books. She waves her hand. That isn't the point, says Therese Quinn of Monroe.

This is a story the mother wants to tell:

It was December 1980. She had been worried about her boy, Jesse O'Reilly. At 9 years old, he was a sweet kid, loved to talk around the kitchen table, enjoyed collecting baseball cards. To the outside world, though, he was shy and cautious and physically frail. Jesse wasn't the type of kid to jump off monkey bars. Therese thought maybe her son should be a little more this way, a little less that way. You know, he should be just right.

That winter, frail Jesse started getting high fevers. He caught everything that was going around school and then some. The doctors couldn't find anything.

His allergies worsened and he acquired new ones. He got abdominal pains. What's wrong, she asked the doctors? His immune system is shot. It's nothing, they told her, you're overwrought.

She was a mother and she knew something was wrong.

By the end of 1981, the doctors found a tumor in Jesse's stomach the size of a cantaloupe.

Within a few months, they took out most of the boy's stomach. The wound won't heal, said the doctor. We can't stop the bleeding.

The mother asked the doctor: Are you trying to tell me my son is going to die?

The doctor nodded. She told him he was crazy.

In the following months, Jesse screamed in pain. He couldn't absorb nutrition. He was hooked to a machine. He was withdrawing from morphine. He endured chemotherapy.

The mother could not think without falling apart, so she did not allow herself to think. A mother's instinct took over. She stayed with him night and day, giving him comfort. When the stomach healed, she called it a miracle.

And when the cancer disappeared, she called that a miracle, too.

Jesse still had to be hooked up to a machine 14 hours a day where he would be shot full of pre-digested food. It always seemed like he was going back to the hospital for one thing or another.

For the next seven years, mother and son took life five minutes at a time.

Instead of feeling nothing, the mother felt everything. The littlest things gave her pleasure. Seeing her boy play baseball. Bringing friends home. Each and every morning seemed like a gift.

Last year was a wonderful year. Jesse became a real teenager, a 16-year-old talking to girls on the phone, going out with friends, even getting caught smoking in the bathroom. He volunteered at Arden Hill, cheering up the kids on the pediatric ward.

In November, Jesse caught pneumonia. That's when the doctors noticed his liver was failing. He was very sick. He was sent to a Pittsburgh hospital to wait for a transplant.

The boy whose spirit of adventure she once questioned said, "C'mon, Mom, let's go. I'm not afraid to die."

The mother believed there would be another miracle.

At the hospital in Pittsburgh, Jesse's kidneys began to fail. So did his lungs and his heart. Two weeks ago, they finally stabilized Jesse enough to perform the transplant.

The doctor came out of the operating room after a few hours and said, it doesn't look good. Jesse was bleeding heavily.

Therese had heard that before. There would be a miracle again. Six hours later, the doctor came out again. "I'm sorry," he said. "His heart just gave out."

She packed his things and headed home. Save for the funeral last week, she hasn't been out of her house.

"You grow a child inside you," she said. "You give birth. Now he's gone. I have an emptiness, an ache inside me I can't describe."

She says all along she was asking for miracles and now she finally understands about such things.

"The miracle was Jesse," she says.

That is the story she says she wants people to know.

"I want them to know what I've learned. Forget all those little anxieties, the petty arguments. They're nonsense. Just get up in the morning and open your eyes. See the light.

"Because nothing, nothing lasts except the love. That's all that connects the living to the dead."

The mother talks about feeling the son's spirit soaring. Her gray eyes shine, taking on life.

Chapter 2:

Humorous Columns

"Everybody has a talent. Mine is having the timing of a $2 watch, with an ability to predict the immediate future that rivals Custer."   — Mike Levine, 1988

Slob Stories

I received the following poignant letter from 11-year-old Stephanie Carnes of Newburgh:

"I am writing about my dad's car. My dad leaves half-full coffee cups on the seats. He says, 'Steph, why do you leave all your coffee cups on the seats?' Yeah, right. I don't drink coffee. The car is littered with everything and it smells like sour milk. My dad doesn't throw stuff in the back seat. He shoves it under the seats. I am afraid to look under the seats.

"My dad's car is the messiest in Orange County. I am drowning in garbage."

Yes, Stephanie, there is a vacuum. But we must save it for the absolute messiest car in the three counties. The competition is overflowing.

Welcome to the results of the Clean Up My Mess Contest, where the winner gets a free $129.95 top-to-bottom, inside-and-out professional cleaning.

It all started when Japanese officials explained away faulty seat belts by saying Americans were so messy, they were lousing up the belts.

There was a howl of patriotic outrage. How dare they call us messy. I pointed out that the Japanese were entirely right.

There's nothing Americans don't do in our automobiles. Eat, sleep, kiss, study, listen to music, warehouse, whatever. We've got the whole world in our cars.

My own Ford Escort is filled with wads of melted Bazooka, Diet Coke stains, piles of papers, mounds of old lunches, old Woodstock passes, defeated Pine Tree air fresheners and, for some reason I can't explain, a soiled 15-year-old winter coat. That's just the front seat.

The trouble with all this messiness is we can't find anything. That's why the Japanese are so far ahead of us. They haven't lost the keys to success under the car seat.

It was time to set messy America on the path to success.

I received a messy pile of sad slob stories. Unfortunately, I put many of them in my car to read later. I am sure I will find them someday when I am searching under the seats for toll booth change.

The responses were great because, unlike the compulsively clean, all messy people have a sense of humor. We had seasoned pros vying for the big prize. But the winner is a 20-year-old rookie messaholic by the name of Elizabeth Shaffner.

Ms. Shaffner's 1989 V.W. Jetta won for pure all-around mess (see her letter). She will receive the $129.95 deluxe cleanup treatment from Crystal Clean Soft Car Wash in Middletown.

As for young Stephanie, I was going to award her dad a free vacuum. But when I called, she told me she already cleaned the car for him, for money. That's cheap, Stephanie.

If I gave her the mailing list of our entrants, she could pay for college.

Slovenly sedans

The messy car as conceptual art ... In which an organized teacher discovers new lessons in creativity.

"Since I teach K-12, I have everything in my car, from glue, glitter, crayons and pencils. Recently, I noticed that a white jacket I wore had black spots on the back. After much investigating, I discovered that a crayon had melted between the seat and seat back. A diet Coke I had in the car too long seeped through the paper cup and filled the compartment where I threw loose change and things. Before I had a chance to clean it up, it dried. Recently, desperate for gas money, I had to pry the change apart and wash it."

— Victoria Hazel, New Paltz

The messy car as therapy ... In which a super-organized single mom and insurance claims adjuster finds a place to let it all hang out.

"My secret spot where I can get away from it all, not be observed or judged, is my wheels. Where else can a well-respected professional suck watermelon cubes and spit the seeds on the floor without having to answer for it? Who is to know that the seeds and old fries have camouflaged the carpet?

"You may locate a vehicle with more inches per square foot of future compost, but I guarantee there is no vehicle in three counties in which the garbage builds up with great fervor and sheer exhilaration."

— Lynn Murray, Montgomery

The messy car as survival tool ... In which a New Windsor woman insists the messy will best survive a nuclear war.

"I see nothing wrong with keeping food under the seats. My car looks like a vending machine exploded, so at least if I were ever stranded in my car I wouldn't starve. This contest gave me the impression that I should clean my car out, but I decided not to because I might need all that stuff some day."

— Jaclyn Peterson, New Windsor

The messy car as historical archive ... In which we preserve.

"Those McDonald's bags have been accumulating since the inception of the drive-thru. I guess I should recycle those newspapers. This one is dated, Aug. 11, 1994. Hey, the Yankees won!"

— Thomas DeStefano, Hamlet of Wallkill.

And the winner:

The messy car as toxic landfill ... In which a rookie messaholic steals the prize for constructing her very own environmental disaster.

"Dear Mike,

"My car is by far the most disgusting in Orange and all surrounding counties. No one but my dog, who always finds moldy and rotten treats, will step foot or paw inside my 1989 Volkswagen Jetta. I cannot even force my teenage brother to borrow it. I have honestly not had a single passenger inside my car since last summer, when I found hundreds of maggots squirming throughout my car's interior.

"I found them while I was searching for a missing article of clothing. Underneath the piles of dirty, smelly socks, wet beach towels and garbage galore, I found them slithering all over rotten McDonald's cheeseburgers, loose fries, and spilled chocolate shakes... That was the first and only time I cleaned my car.

"After a storm my car is like a rainforest. Water pours through the floor vents, and my entire passenger side floor is covered in anywhere from 3-5 inches of water. The water mixes with the dirty clothes, moldy food, cigarette butts, snotty tissues, magazines, Q-Tips and anything and everything else imaginable, and turns into a sewer. Any normal person would sort through and vacuum it out. I just leave the window open for a few days until the water evaporates. The smell that is left behind would deter any life form and cannot be masked by any perfume or air-freshener.

"Every piece of important paperwork has found its way to the floor and has been destroyed in the floods. I was going to send a picture but my camera is lost inside somewhere, and I am not about to look because I fear what else I might find. My seats are stained brown and there is not an inch of empty floor space. My boyfriend made me tint my windows because he wants no one to know what a pig I really am.

"My ashtray is overflowing. There is not even room for a stale piece of gum, so it's stuck all over the dashboard. Please, Mike, help me! And please contact me if there is ever a contest for messiest bedroom. It's even worse than my car. Thank you.

"This is all true; I even have eyewitnesses. And believe it or not there's a lot more I could tell you, but I just cannot stomach anymore, and I'm sure you can't, either."

Elizabeth Schaffner, Newburgh

Real Men Aren't Afraid of Cramps

The newsroom just received a big box from Procter & Gamble Co. It says, "Get Ready To Taste History." Rip it open, stop the presses, this could be the breakthrough America has been panting for.

Inside were two teeny foil bags. One was marked "regular potato chips." The other was labeled "fat-free potato chips made with Olean brand fat replacer"

Being hard-boiled reporters, we reacted dispassionately.

"Oooh, let me see. No, me first. Wow, cool, no fat, tastes good, gonna change everything."

Not since the release of "Sgt. Pepper's Lonely Hearts Club Band" have baby boomers so eagerly greeted a new arrival. We had copped some olestra before it hit the stores. Potato chips without fat that had, in the words of Procter & Gamble "no taste trade-off."

We needed to set up a readers' taste test pronto.

Wait a minute, said someone, read the warning label:

"This product contains olestra. Olestra may cause abdominal cramping and loose stools. Olestra inhibits the absorption of some vitamins and other nutrients..."

Dead silence.

Well, maybe we shouldn't try it on our readers, cautioned one editor.

Come on, I said, this is FDA approved. Our government wouldn't steer us wrong, would they? Gimme those bags.

I went out asking people at random if they wanted to try the new fat-free chips.

Sure, they said. Then I read them the warning label. No thanks, they said.

Taste it yourself, the managing editor told me. All right, sir. Real men aren't afraid of cramps.

I enlisted a fellow-taster in veteran Record tastemeister Chris Farlekas. Chris and I come from the old school of journalism — we will do anything for food.

But why was this olestra supposed to be the greatest thing since sliced bread?

Because, we were told, it gives you the taste of fat without it being absorbed in your bloodstream. Goes right out. Unfortunately, it takes water soluble vitamins along with it and perhaps half your breakfast.

I asked people at Procter & Gamble about this. They told me their olestra products will contain vitamins to replace those that are lost.

What about the diarrhea and cramps? In perfect corporatese, they referred to these as "common digestive effects."

"It's like with fruits and vegetables" said a spokesman, "and some high-fiber cereals."

Um, not really. Fruits and vegetables are high-fiber. Olestra chips have the same scant amount of fiber as regular potato chips.

And the taste? "One hundred percent taste," said the corporate hand-out.

I had to find out myself. After all, this is a company that gave us Pringles, a chip that has all the down-home taste of balsa wood. The word is P&G will be putting out Pringles with olestra.

Chris and I were given samples of the regular chips and the fat-free chips.

Both tasted OK, but we each correctly picked out the regular chips. Fried in real oil, they had that greasy, stop-your-heart zing America loves.

The olestra-fried chips weren't bad. Compare it to decent decaf coffee vs. the real thing. However, the roof of my mouth tasted like my saliva had just been replaced by synthetic motor oil; maybe it was my imagination.

And maybe so were the cramps that sent me dashing for safe haven. I mean it could have been on account of the Yodels I had before the chips. Farlekas, who writes sonnets about cheese cake, felt no side effects.

Procter & Gamble said they would be test marketing Olean chips during the next several months. No, it couldn't say exactly where. It should be here soon enough.

Judge for yourself. In case Procter & Gamble wants my personal testimonial, here it is:

"Olean fat-free chips: Bet you can only eat one."

It's Just a Dog...It's Just a Dog...Really

April 16, 1989

I was thinking about getting a dog.

Big deal, right?

That's what I said to myself. At least until I happened to mention it to other people.

Gee whiz. It's like I'm embarking on some monumental rite of passage, filled with deep meaning. Not even when I got married did I get this much heart-to-heart advice. Dogs must be the most emotionally charged symbol in America.

President Bush talks about the budget deficit or his grandchildren and everyone yawns. But when his dog has puppies, the world stops.

When my wife and I told people we were having a baby, they said, "that's nice." But when I mention I might be getting a dog, they perk up. "A dog?" they exclaim. "Well, let me tell you...!"

The first person I spoke to said wanting a dog spoke volumes about my place in middle-class culture.

"Getting a dog, eh?" she cackled. "That does it. First the kids, then the house, the station wagon and now the dog. A dog. Boy, you've really done it. What next? A Sears card? Plaid golf pants?"

Wow, I get one mutt and I'm Ozzie Nelson.

Then there's this whole other group of people who told me my life was now complete.

"Dogs are more than your best friend," gushed this group. "They're family. And you'll be doing your kids a favor. A dog will teach them about loyalty. A dog will teach them about giving. A dog will teach them the true meaning of love."

Great. Let the dogs pay for the kids' college education.

Then, there was the "you'll be sorry" gang.

"Wait till you mow the lawn and you find the hidden dog doo. The furniture will be a mess, their hair will be all over everything, the house will reek. They're as demanding as children. You'll never be able to go away. In two weeks, even the kids will hate the dog. You're ruining your life."

All of a sudden I'm nervous about this dog business, like this is a major life decision.

Maybe there's some way out, I hoped, as we headed up to the Mamakating shelter.

At first, I thought I had an ally in our 3-year-old son. He has only recently accepted the fact that we weren't returning his 7-month-old brother Sam to the hospital where he was born. What did he want with more competition?

But Ben was positively cheerful about a new arrival. "And if we get two dogs," he said, "we won't have any room left for Sammy."

We go to the shelter in Mamakating.

Out comes Becky, a mutt who recently gave birth to 11 puppies. She has no home.

Ol' Becky is not a show dog. She's part collie, part lab and maybe part woodchuck. No matter.

My wife turns to Jell-O and gives a joyous look I thought was reserved only for the judge pronouncing us husband and wife.

"She reminds me of Tiny," she says, with a catch in her voice. Tiny was her childhood dog she still talks about.

Then Becky came over to me, hopped up and nestled her head against my chest.

Then my wife and I did what parents do when they want something for themselves.

We said, "Let's do it for the kids."

So Becky's coming to live with us in a couple of weeks.

Not that we're treating it like any major event.

OK. So we already brought a leash and my wife is making a special dog bed. So we're planning a big welcoming party. So Ben is already dreaming about her and I'm already thinking about fencing in the yard to make it safer and more fun for the mutt.

But, hey, she's just a dog.

I don't know why other people make such a big deal about them.

You Know, It's Akin to Washing Your Car

August 12, 1988

"No relief in sight," says the Kingston TV weather forecaster.

"Humid, in the 90s for the foreseeable future," says the guy on the 24-hour weather channel.

Any day, now, expect the geek weatherman on Channel 9 to scream, "Helllllloooooo, Armageddon!"

Sure feels like it. As you read this, another scorcher is rising in the east, with a sickly green sky that looks like it's been flown in from Jersey City. Eight a.m. in the mid-Hudson feels like high noon in hell.

Oh, I know what they say. No sense in talking about the weather; you can't do anything about it.

I can. At least I'm going to take a shot at ending this heat wave. For the good of the human race. For the good of the lovely Lorraine Levine, who is in her ninth month of pregnancy and has developed some highly original adjectives to describe heat.

Hey, I'm not claiming it's going to be easy to end this summerlong firestorm. I don't have any celestial connections. I don't even know Oral Roberts.

But I do have one weapon.

Whenever I write a column that's tied to the weather, it always backfires.

If I talk about snow, the sun comes out. If I write about spring, a blizzard forms over the Catskills. So maybe if I write about it being hotter than Hades, it'll cool off.

Call it dumb luck with the accent on dumb. Strictly as a public service, I present my awesome track record:

In October of 1983, I write a mood column about the chill of autumn. The day it appears, the thermometer hits 92 degrees.

June 1984: I write a column about the joys of summer. The day the article runs, you have to wear an overcoat.

February 1985: The weather forecasters said a major snowstorm will arrive by morning "without fail." I cancel a political column I have prepared for the next day and ride around the mid-Hudson interviewing adults who secretly love snow. I run breathlessly back to my office and type in the column on deadline.

Three cheers for Frosty the Columnist. The next morning, readers open to a column about how the snow must be piling up on their windows. The only problem is the sun is shining. Not a flake of snow has fallen or is about to.

Then in September '85 came Hurricane Gloria. Well, everyone said it was coming. I listened to the guy from the National Hurricane Center the day before. Gloria's coming right at us, he said. Winds topping 80 mph, torrential rains, terrible destruction.

Oh, I wrote a wonderful Hurricane Gloria column. It landed on readers' doorsteps just as the hurricane was supposed to hit the New York area. "As you read this," I wrote, "rain is pounding the area. Winds are bending mighty oak trees. Batten down the hatches."

Very dramatic, except for one thing. Hurricane Gloria had dropped dead in Atlantic City. Here in the mid-Hudson, it drizzled until noon. The wind didn't even bend a blade of grass.

Some readers think this reflects on my ability to be wrong about nearly everything. A few have reminded me that at the beginning of this year, I assured Record readers that the Democratic ticket would be Sam Nunn and Bill Bradley. I wrote that Dole would crush Bush in the primaries.

Hey, who cares? Everybody has a talent. Mine is having the timing of a $2 watch, with an ability to predict the immediate future that rivals Custer.

I just hope I can put this perverse talent to good use in helping to end this heat wave. Just by writing a column about the heat, a cold front will start kicking down from Canada. Any day now. Any day.

Failure, don't fail me now.

...And Lo, a Voice Spoke, and It Was Good: Shamefaced Deadcrops, Arise, Fertilize

March 12, 1995

I am a descendent of the ancient tribe known as the Deadcrops.

This tribe, which sprung up around 570 B.C. on the Isle of Canasta, was unable to grow anything from the soil. The Deadcrops failed at wheat, corn, rutabagas and, finally, stinkweed.

Many Deadcrops perished in the Great Seven Year Itch, when tribe members mistook poison sumac for aloe vera.

Facing starvation, the Deadcrops ended up inventing plastic fruit, settled in the Bronx and found rent-controlled apartments.

For generations, they lived happily in the city, unaware of their Deadcrop roots. But, yea, in the last half of the 20th century, the Deadcrops left the Bronx and moved up to the fertile Hudson Valley.

Here, they were surrounded by lush lawns, blossoming gardens, ripe fruits and fresh vegetables.

Facing suburban peer pressure, the Deadcrops tried their incompetent darndest. But they remained hopelessly faithful to their rotted roots.

Not one blade of grass grew from a Deadcrop lawn. Not one radish survived in a native Deadcrop garden. The closest we got to raising a single corn was on our sore feet.

With another growing season arriving, I am hereby calling for a convention of the Deadcrop tribe. We must learn how to grow, or perish in peer shame.

The first step on the road to recovery is: Don't be ashamed to admit your ancestry. We Deadcrops have given the world plenty — artificial flowers, patio furniture, Calydryl.

In return, we have endured shame for our bald lawns. We have been hooted out of Agways across the valley.

Year after year, I subject myself to humiliation by recounting my earnest efforts to grow one blade of grass.

No more.

I will stand up and say it out loud. My name is Mike and I am a Deadcrop. I am going to grow a living thing this year.

This should be easy to do in the Hudson Valley, where pollen hangs over us like the London fog. So I called the Cooperative Extensions in Orange, Sullivan and Ulster. They were very encouraging.

"Try tomatoes," said Susan Rondinaro, horticulture agent for the Cooperative Extension. "If you can't grow tomatoes, you might as well hang it up."

Alrighty. Tomatoes it will be. I am looking for five other members of the Deadcrop tribe to join me in this great task.

Together we will grow one tomato plant. It will be big, it will be juicy, it will be eaten. From seed to salad, we will grow this plant under the supervision of our local Cooperative Extensions, armed with a team of experts.

This is our big chance to show the world we deserve to breathe. I am sending out a call to Deadcrops everywhere. Tell me about your Deadcrop roots, your humiliation, your secret pride.

How do you know if you are a true surviving member of the Deadcrops? There are three requirements:

1. You have been unable to grow anything edible or aesthetically pleasing.

2. You have a bare lawn, or at least one dead plant in your house.

3. You are so ignorant about gardening that you think 'hoe' is a nasty word.

Send me your names and phone numbers. I will get back to you and set up a secret meeting place (someplace indoors, I guarantee you). We will elect five tribal members to grow a tomato.

Naturally, we will take a big photograph to show the world the Deadcrops ain't dead.

C'mon, you have nothing to lose but your Deadcrop shame. If your tribe can't grow a tomato, we can always try casino gambling.

Better Not Mess Around With This Revolution

I was working at my desk when I saw my boss standing above me smiling.

Perhaps he was there to tell a funny joke. Maybe he would compliment me on a column. Could this be the raise I had been hoping for?

Then I looked closer and I recognized the wicked smile he had pasted on his face. It's a cruel grimace that's been flashed by every neataholic who rules this world.

Looking down at my desk and dripping with sadistic glee, he said, "It's time to clean your desk."

My boss does this every couple of months. Then I have to go pile the contents of my desk into 10 Hefty lawn bags and cart them off to my basement to collect mildew.

I do this because it's a neataholic world. Why can't I build a pile of messiness up to the ceiling, I asked my boss?

"You have to understand," he said. "It's not that we mind you living like a human scumball. We have to worry about the environmental impact on your colleagues, OSHA regulations, fire safety."

That's a typical bureaucratic response of the ruling neataholic culture. Well, I've had it.

Hear ye. Hear ye. This is a call to arms to every messy person.

Messiness is not a failing. It is a lifestyle choice.

Every messy soul who's tired of being held under the thumb of the oppressive neataholic culture, rise up and revolt.

Say it loud. We're messy and we're proud.

We're sloppy and we're hoppy.

(See, we don't even have to rhyme neatly.)

For years, messiness has been treated like a fault, a weakness, a shame.

Moralists cluck at us. Why? I don't see anything in the Ten Commandments poo-pooing a messy lifestyle.

Psychologists discriminate against us. They say sloppiness is our attempt to create chaos in order to avoid dealing with real issues in our lives.

That's a typical lie of the oppressive neataholic culture. Messy people simply have better things to do than put recipes in alphabetical order.

Yessir, I've been collecting studies on neat people. I can't find them at the moment but it's somewhere on my desk. Oh, here it is.

One study says people with clean desks are rigid control freaks. They run the world.

Beware of the person with the cleanest work space. They're up to no good.

Hitler's desk was spotless. Mussolini was crazed about perfectly sharpened pencils.

Messy people wouldn't start a war. We're too busy looking for our lost dry-cleaning ticket.

Studies also show neataholics are no fun. They're prone to cheapness. They're nags. They never slide into second. They worry about getting the stain out.

They're 10 times more prone to heart disease.

Why don't we ever hear about that? Because the media is neataholic-dominated, dedicated to organizing this chaotic world into some daily laughable order.

Sorry, boss, I'm proud to say my desk is bursting with the random energy of life. Chinese food, coffee, old bologna sandwiches, saltines, the ghost of Elvis. That same work space has stacks of papers, all of which have been thoughtfully saved from landing in the overflowing county landfill.

It's randomly decorated with a child's baseball glove, an invitation to a 1984 Christmas party, a pair of extra socks, a can of sliced peaches, notes from a 1983 Lumberland board meeting. Back in the '70s, the FBI searched my desk for Patty Hearst.

Neataholics run the planet. But just wait.

Someday, we will take over. We'll make neataholics leave coffee rings on their desk. We'll force them to de-alphabetize their address book. We'll take away their files, their photocopying machines, their five-year plans, their...

Editor's note: Unless he cleans off his desk, Levine will be packed inside a Hefty bag and be filed under "U" for unemployed. Watch this space for further developments

Oh Rats, Mickey Mouse

I have vacation time coming up this month.

My family wants to go to Disney World.

I could have said we can't afford it, which is true. I could have said every motel room south of Newark is booked during the holidays. This is also true.

But I decided to stand up tall and say from the bottom of my heart that I loathe Disney World. I said I would rather spend my vacation at the Harriman tollbooths.

Mouths dropped. My eldest son is looking for an 800 number to report me. My wife is probably on the phone to a lawyer.

They have even told neighbors and friends about my anti-Disney World sentiments. The community now stares at me like I'm a flag-burner.

I've discovered that not wanting to go to Disney World is against the law in America. You have to go and you have to like it. They make winning Super Bowl quarterbacks scream, "Now that I won the Super Bowl, I'm going to Disney World!" as they trot off the field.

I dream of winning the Super Bowl so I can look America in the eye and say, "I'd rather collect Spam recipes than go to Disney World."

What's wrong with Disney World? Nothing. It feels about as adventurous as eating at McDonald's. Everything is pre-processed, pre-experienced, market-tested. There are all these people saying have a nice day and not meaning it.

Then they hit on me to buy some T-shirt or video game celebrating some jive occasion like Mickey's 60th birthday.

I went to Disneyland in California when I was a teenager. I was expecting something fun like Palisades Park, where you eat greasy French fries, chase your friends and get sick on top of the Ferris wheel.

Instead, I got to stand on long lines with whiney kids. Their parents spent $5,000 to have the kids say they're tired and they want to go back to the motel room and watch TV. Three days and three nights just to work your way through a few rides.

Then the ride started, a trip down Pioneer Land or something, narrated by a 19-year-old Dick Clark lookalike so squeaky clean, he appeared to be scrub-brushed with Comet. What I wouldn't have given to be in the Crazy House at Coney Island wolfing down Nathan's hot dogs.

Then I had to contend with some squirt dressed up as Mickey Mouse. Don't start with that animal. It's time America came clean about Mickey Mouse. He's not funny. He has the personality of Ed McMahon. He's a rodent.

Of course, when it comes to Disney World, getting there is half the fun.

You can fly for $1,000 a family. Or for a real treat, take the family car and enjoy a pleasant 25-hour ride. Your family is really ready for fun when you get out of that car. Anyone still talking to each other? Good, then you can chat as you walk to Disney World from your parking space in the next county.

I'm told some couples go to Disney World on their honeymoon. I don't understand that. I really don't. Nothing like an 8-foot rodent to put you in a romantic mood.

I thought my wife knew I hated Disney World before we married. I confessed my theme park phobia on our second date. I had to come clean with her before our relationship got serious.

She said she understood but that she was sure I'd change my mind if I ever became a father.

I have children. I have a station wagon. I have a dog.

I will not go to Disney World.

I said I've never traveled. I've never even been to Canada. Sue me, but if we get a few bucks to travel I don't want to bozo around with Goofy.

Aw, c'mon party pooper, I'm told, the kids will love Disney World.

Hey, kids like lots of things. They like giving noogies, the quarter rides in front of Playtogs, sticking straws up their noses. Let 'em enjoy that.

But it is of no use. My oldest boy won't let up.

I finally told him we can't go to Disney World. There are alligators there. They will eat us up.

His mom told him daddy is only kidding. She said, in fact, that if we don't meet Donald Duck in person within the next few years, it will be daddy who will be devoured by alligators.

Oh well, it's better than going to Disney World.

Oh Well, There Goes the Neighborhood

Big deal, my friends tell me, so you're married. So you've got a couple of kids to feed, clothe and put through college. So you have 42 payments left on a car that's already sucking wind.

So what, they tell me. You're still traveling with a light suitcase until you buy a house.

"Now there's commitment," say my friends. "You won't be such a wiseguy when the mortgage is due."

Well, that's just fine, fellas, I tell them, 'cause I ain't never buying a house. I grew up in the city. I know about kick-starting apartment-house elevators and banging on the super's door when there's no heat. Houses, I know from nothing. Don't even care to.

Anyway, I tell them, I can't even begin to afford a home. Case closed.

I bought a house yesterday.

I am still in shock from the closing. If there is anybody in Orange County I didn't write out a check to yesterday, please let me know, and I'll dash one off as soon as my hand heals.

I am also still in shock from the generosity of our family and friends who made this move possible.

They will live to regret their kindness. In fact, the whole mid-Hudson will live to regret their generosity because you can bet if Levine buys a house, real estate is no longer a sound investment.

I am allergic to money. I have never bought anything at the right moment. I'm the guy who buys an eight-cylinder Chevy right before a gas shortage. Now, not only will my infamous sense of timing spell doom for my family, it will cause the entire region's housing market to crash.

I looked for our house at the peak of the boom, a good five years after the last house in Orange County flew out of my price range. A week after our bid on the house was accepted, I read an article in Business Monday about the slump in housing prices.

When we applied for our mortgage, we were quoted a going interest rate. Of course, said our friendly banker, that rate could go up by the time your mortgage is approved, but that's unlikely. "Mortgage rates have stayed steady for 10 months now," he said.

Within a week after we applied, mortgage rates across America went up. We got socked.

That's all that should concern you other homeowners — a certain downfall in your property values and rising interest rates.

The rest is my problem. The sellers were nice enough to let us move in before the closing. It took us two days to move — it rained both days. After it stopped raining, it turned cold.

Wonderful. I moved into a house just in time to rake leaves and turn on the heat.

And now I'm really lost.

The seller showed me all this maintenance-type stuff I've already forgot. The seller is in South Carolina. I do remember one thing— I'm supposed to change the filter on the furnace.

First thing I did in the house was go down to the basement to pull the old filter out. I can't find it. I'm not even sure which one's the furnace and which one's the water heater.

My wife, who grew up in a house in Circleville, is the resident expert (just one more thing she's smarter than me about). She knows just how often she wants the lawn mowed next spring and she knows who's going to do it.

That's not all. I now take a lunchbox to work and buy Foodtown brand everything. I canceled Cinemax.

Truth is I'm not complaining too hard. We have a modest house on a pleasant street in an old railroad city where the boxcars no longer run.

For eight years, I've debated whether I should follow that last train out of Middletown. Something about this place got a hold on me but I don't know what it is.

I do know that, as of yesterday, I'm not a tourist in this town, anymore. And if I can ever find where the furnace filter is, we might even make a life of it.

Lines From Diary of a Mad Homeowner

City boys like us, baby, we were born to rent. To call the super in times of trouble. To play stoopball with the kid from Apt. 5C. To bang the pipes when there is no heat.

I rented when I moved up here. I was perfectly happy.

I was made to feel like a criminal. Didn't I know I was guilty of throwing my money away? Guilty of depriving my kids? Guilty of not building up equity?

I crumbled last fall and bought a house. I am keeping a journal of this blessed life passage. It's called Diary of a Mad Homeowner. Each month starts with a line I heard about the advantages of owning a home:

October: "You won't be throwing away your money, anymore." I must write a check to everyone in Orange County. Most other states would call it extortion. New York calls it a house closing. Our family celebrates by checking newspaper ads for macaroni and cheese coupons.

November: "You'll really enjoy owning a piece of God's good earth." I used to relax on the weekends. Now I am a human rake. I rake all day and the next morning, 4 million more leaves appear. I hate trees. Why do they torture me?

December: All the leaves have finally fallen. The bare trees reveal our backyard view: Middletown's biggest cemetery. It brightens up our every morning.

The first slushstorm. I am a smart guy to buy a house on a hilltop. Our car's skidding journey down the icy slope looks like one of those Wide World of Sports shots when the announcer says, "And the agony of defeat." Crash.

January: "You can turn the heat up as high as you want." We awake to a cold house. My wife sends me down to the basement to straighten this out. I turn on the light, look at the furnace and declare, "Yep, it's not working." We call a heating guy. "Ha, ha," says the good-natured serviceman. "The pilot light is out. You see, you just have to pull a switch." Ha ha, it's $42. Then he pats our furnace and says, "Nice antique."

February: "You can make repairs when you want." We wake up to a flooded basement. It's the water heater. Ha ha, says the good-natured heating man. Oh good, I think, it's just a switch again. No, this time it's $400. My credit union loan line looks like the national deficit.

March: "Owning a home is a great investment." In October, mid-Hudson real estate prices had been skyrocketing for five years. As I am allergic to money, I knew I would put a stop to this trend. Since I bought my house, area real estate prices have actually declined.

April: "You'll see the seasons come alive before your very eyes." Our front yard tree has no buds. It looks dead as a telephone poll. We better cut it down, I say. Mrs. Levine informs me a tree surgeon costs more than a brain surgeon. Dead trees look nice, I say. Less raking.

May: "Wait until the weather gets nice, you'll really enjoy your home." Thanks to the water heater, our planned week's vacation in the country becomes one night in Scranton. The whole time I worry about my lawn.

It is the ugliest lawn in the universe, a combination of weeds and bald spots. I imagine the neighbors staring at the windows, passing by, going, "Shame, shame on the Levines."

But I have good neighbors. They do not talk behind my back. One looked me in the eye and told me my lawn looked like the Ho Chi Minh Trail.

I buy grass seed. I drop it on the ground. I didn't know I was supposed to use topsoil. Because it has rained for the last 40 days, it grows anyway. But it is a different shade than the rest of the grass. My lawn looks like a Pittsburgh Paint color chart for the green family.

June: "And every kid needs a back yard." My 3-year-old loves subways. But he is convinced our back yard is inhabited by gorillas and lions and a monster who wants to eat Middletown, starting with our house.

I'm not so sure he's wrong. The cat just brought in a snake. We have wasps the size of Buicks. The tree I thought should be cut down has more leaves than the Black Forest. I am already looking forward to the fall raking.

Only 353 monthly payments to go and the house is ours. I will be 66 years old. The first thing we will do is move to an apartment. Maybe the kid from 5C will still want to play stoopball.

See the Cookie Crumble

So there I was in Gardiner, bent over a stove, a personal slave to complete strangers.

Cooking their dinner. Cleaning their kitchen. Feeding their dog, for crying out loud.

This is what I deserve for having a BIG MOUTH.

It all started when I announced a "Busiest Person of the Mid-Hudson" contest. I said I would buy and cook dinner for the winner.

Meanwhile, the busy winner would get to take some time and relax.

We got dozens of harried replies, but the winner was Sharon Formisano. She's a junior high English teacher, a single mother of four boys ages 12 to 17, a producer of school plays, an active member of community groups, a chauffeur for the kids, a laundress, a cook... you get the picture.

Okey-dokey, Ms. Formisano, I announced, walking in with my groceries for dinner, you just relax today and let me do all the work.

Can you believe this woman? She took me at my word.

I have never seen such relaxation in my life. Ms. Formisano slumped on a couch and vegged out on Donahue. "This is the first time I've watched TV in months," she said. Her kids were sprawled out, too, sprung from helping mom.

Me, I was chopping, slicing, sweating over a hot sauce, my big mouth opened with exhaustion.

Don't offer to help even a little, I panted, I'll do everything myself.

OK, she said.

OK, said the kids, don't forget to feed the dog.

Meanwhile, I had 12-year-old Kenny peering over my shoulder watching me make meatballs. "Looks interesting," he said with great politeness.

Ah, the meatballs. My moment of truth had arrived.

I can cook all right in a bachelor sort of way. As for big main meals for company, I can make two dishes. One is a good homemade spaghetti sauce and the other isn't.

What I cannot do is stuff that has to be perfectly timed like roast beef. But with today's busy lifestyles, who eats roast beef anymore?

So when Sharon Formisano won the contest, I called her and asked, "What does your family want to eat, ma'am? You can have anything."

"We want roast beef," Ms. Formisano said.

"Fine," I said as my stomach went weak. "How about some spaghetti sauce on the side."

"OK," she said, "the kids like spaghetti."

"Great," I said, "then let's forget the roast beef and have a big ol' spaghetti dinner."

I threw in meatballs and we had a deal.

I started the sauce the day before. It's a family recipe passed down by my father who's as Italian as Milton Berle. Sue me, it tastes great.

As for meatballs, so what if I had never made them before.

I walked into the supermarket, stood next to the ground beef and asked out loud, "Hey, anyone know how to make meatballs?" A young guy told me how. The secret he said is don't pack the meatballs too hard.

That's basically all I remembered the next day at the Formisanos. I mixed some eggs, bread crumbs and anything within arm's reach. And then I said to myself, the guy said don't pack them too hard.

I packed them real loose and started browning them in a frying pan. I put in enough olive oil to create an oil slick. Then I threw it all in the perfectly good sauce.

The meatballs started coming apart.

Uh oh. I hatched an emergency plan.

Only when everyone looked desperately famished, I called them to the table. Two of her children had lame excuses for skipping dinner, which I didn't accept.

There's nothing like a good spaghetti dinner, said Sharon Formisano.

And that's what the Formisanos had. Nothing like a good spaghetti dinner.

"The garlic bread is good," said Ms. Formisano.

The kids kept their heads down. They were polite without lying. The sauce was good, they said.

Nobody said anything about the meatballs or meat clumps or meat objects or whatever they could be called.

I had really made a mess in the kitchen. I didn't know where to begin. Oh, that's all right, I said looking pitiful, I'll clean it up.

Great, said the Formisanos.

So I cleaned, I scrubbed, I swept, I prepared dessert and cleaned that up, too.

It was all worth it, said Sharon Formisano, meatballs and all. She said she hasn't sat down for this long in many a day.

Gee, too bad she was going to be up all night.

The Party's Shaping Up

March 4, 1990

It's over. Yippee. Party time!

February may have lasted only 28 days, but for those of us in the "I Hate to Exercise Club," this was the longest month in God's creation.

As one seething club member pointed out, it's all my fault. I started this mess. I had the bright idea that those of us who hate exercise also deserve to live.

Sure, the thought of aerobics gives us chest pains. Those Reebok-heads in spandex make us nauseous. Nautilus is a torture rack to us.

But we can't duck the truth. Exercising helps people not drop dead. It fights heart disease, stress, circulatory disease and if you believe the latest study, exercise also cuts down our risk of cancer.

All we need to do, say the experts, is exercise vigorously three times a week for 20 minutes.

That really didn't seem too bad. Were we going to let the world be taken over by those Jane Fonda types, winking at themselves in the mirror, measuring their pecs?

The "I Hate to Exercise Club" was born.

We made a pledge. If each of us could exercise three times a week for 20 minutes during the course of a month, we'd throw ourselves a sit-down party. At the party, we'd eat M&Ms and throw the leftovers at a Jane Fonda exercise video.

Nearly 90 readers wrote in to join. We got everyone from teenagers to rabbis to seniors to mothers to a woman recovering from cancer to guys who watch Knicks games over a gallon of Breyer's ice cream.

Of course, members pledged with all the enthusiasm of someone volunteering for a month at Green Haven prison. "I'll do it because there's a party at the end," moaned Kathryn DeBord of Newburgh. Me, too.

I started to exercise at home. I have this stationary bicycle that was built before Jack LaLanne was born. It sounds like a hydraulic hammer and pedals like a rusted tricycle.

Boy, that was hard work. I began to work up a fierce appetite. Before heading for the kitchen, I checked the clock to see how long I had biked. It was a little under four minutes.

I figured I better go to the health club.

As soon as I walked in, I was a marked man. My picture and my column making fun of health clubs had been hung up in the exercise room. Guys the size of Buicks would stare at my mug. Now I know how Jesse James felt walking into a post office.

Some people came over and said I had a lot of misconceptions about exercise. They were right. For instance, I thought a Stairmaster was the most boring exercise machine in the world until they put me on a rowing machine. Also, I don't think I was too good at it.

I hadn't seen this many people avoiding eye contact since I was on the D train at midnight.

Actually, I thought I was doing OK, until I was told I had to improve my heart rate. It wasn't right for my age. I had a heart rate appropriate for George Burns.

I kept chugging along, waiting for that exercise "high" I was promised. The only high I got was when I started to hallucinate some fried egg rolls. I could hardly wait for this month to end.

Then I talked to Janet Herzberg, executive director of the America Heart Association of Orange, Sullivan and Rockland. She said she was really proud of the club. "This is so wonderful," she gushed. Of course, said Ms. Herzberg, the benefits of exercise disappear quickly if you don't keep at it.

You mean we can't just do it for a month?

"It's a lifetime commitment," she said. "Har-de-har-har-har."

Aw, c'mon, that's not fair. But the awful truth is I am going to continue this exercise stuff. I am going to join — I can't believe I am writing this — the health club.

It wasn't the health nuts who got me to continue. Or even Ms. Herzberg's sound advice. It was the regular people I met who said because they exercise, they basically eat what they want. Every time they get an ache, they don't suspect it is the beginning of a heart attack. They feel like, God willing, they will get to see their grandchildren.

We'll swap more stories at our party, which will be an open house at the Levines. It's BYOJ (Bring Your Own Junk). Date and details will be mailed within the next two weeks. If you hung in there reasonably well with your pledge, come join the party.

The door prize is my rusty stationary bike.

Six Months and Still Going Smokeless

June 9, 1985

I did something smart for a change last fall. I decided to try to quit smoking.

Than I did something very stupid. I announced it in the column.

Come Dec. 1, *wrote Loudmouth Levine*, I will no longer smoke. You can bet on it.

Wonderful! I now had 80,000 potential spies checking up on me. If I failed, I would hear about it for the rest of my days.

"Oh, you're the weak-willed fool who told the world he would quit smoking," they'd taunt me.

I will say only one thing in my defense. I announced I was quitting in the column only to see if there were any other readers who wanted to join me. I thought I would be performing a public service.

My friends don't buy this. They believe that I simply couldn't keep my big trap shut.

It's an interesting theory.

Still, on Dec. 1, 1984, I, along with 50 other Record readers who called in, quit smoking cigarettes.

For the first month, we cried on each other's shoulders. We sang old cigarette jingles. We snapped at Santa Claus.

Meanwhile, I would meet readers in the supermarket and they would check my pockets for cigarettes. "Smoking yet?" they'd ask suspiciously. One lady even asked to smell my breath.

In January, our no-smoking group ate our way through a party to "celebrate" our quitting. We were like army ants. Only good manners stopped us from chewing on the table. It was pure hell.

Then things got tough.

There was depression, irritation, and weight gains. Would we become the gang that couldn't quit?

Six months later, I am here to say that several of us have made it. Honest, I haven't had one puff of one cigarette. I'm even two pounds lighter than before I quit.

No one from our group has turned into one of those obnoxious reformed-smoker zealots. If smoking wasn't bad for our health, we'd go back to it in a minute. And we don't say we will never smoke again.

For those of you who continue to smoke, we have no lectures. If you got a minute, we do have a small message.

We can imagine how pleasurable smoking can be for you. A cigarette seems like a dependable friend at times. How can you live without it?

It's hard at first to quit. Real hard. But if you give it some time, it gets easier.

You begin to go to bed at night without secretly thinking you're going to die from smoking. You wake up in the morning and you can breathe like a normal human being.

In time, you go for days and weeks without craving a smoke. And then gradually, you come to the realization: You can live without smoking.

You're not stupid. You know that if you continue to smoke, it probably will kill you. You can rationalize that all you want. But there is no getting around it; dying early is a terrifying prospect. Are cigarettes worth it?

We make no claim to any special strength of character because we've managed to quit so far. I, for one, got lucky. If I hadn't found out the night before the first column appeared that my wife and I were expecting a child, I might never have lasted the first week.

No one in our group belongs to the smug health-nut crowd. There will always be ashtrays in my house for smoking visitors. There never will be any lectures.

But if you do decide to quit, feel free to give us a call. We can offer encouragement as well as a few tips that worked for us. Call me at the paper and I'll put you in touch with others in our group.

I never thought I could make it this far. I now believe anyone can quit.

Actually, I have only one piece of rock-solid advice. If you decide to quit, for crying out loud, don't announce it in the newspaper.

For the Lovelorn, Some Stock Advice

June 22, 1983

It's a tough world out there, these days. People have problems that weren't even invented 20 years ago.

That's why the most widely read feature in newspapers is the advice column.

"My husband's second daughter by his fourth wife is getting married to my first husband's male secretary. They want an open marriage but a closed wedding. No one is invited except our family German shepherd, who will be the bridesmaid. The question is, should the pooch bring a guest?"

— Signed, Doggone Puzzled.

Well, it's a good question. Who else would even bother offering a solution except an advice columnist? The more wacky the problem, the more the advice columnists want to take a stab at solving it.

But let's face it — Ann Landers is always solving problems for other people who live in Nebraska or some other planet. What we need is an advice column for local affairs of the heart.

I am unqualified for this lofty task. So I unloaded some of my mail on Dr. Lefty Laughingstock, spiritual adviser to the mid-Hudson.

Dear Dr. Laughingstock,

Help! I am hopelessly in love with an elusive lady named Casino Gambling. If she were here, life would be paradise and all my problems would disappear. But she always seems just out of my reach. The problem is that until she comes, I don't feel

like doing anything. Everything seems futile. I refuse to think about the future without her. I'm cranky and negative and very touchy. What can I do?

— Signed, Mountain Man.

Dear Mountain Man,

When a tough guy like you falls in love, you really do it up. Remember when you fell in love with that woman named Monticello Raceway? You thought she would fix everything. But she didn't. I'm not suggesting you give up on your new love, but you can make life better for yourself in the meantime. Plan your future as if Casino Gambling weren't ever coming. And then if she does, it will be icing on the cake. You're still a good-looking guy, Mountain Man. Believe in yourself.

Dear Dr. Laughingstock,

Nobody in the mid-Hudson loves me. Sure, I'm arrogant. Sure, I want to put power lines across the countryside that will ruin the landscape. And yes, almost all of the electricity generated will go to customers outside the mid-Hudson. Of course, I'll spray herbicides around the power lines.

But is this any reason to hate a guy? I've tried changing my name, but still nobody loves. Poor me.

— Signed, Everyone Still Calls Me PASNY

Dear PASNY,

Tough.

Dear Dr. Laughingstock,

I recently moved to Orange County and now all I do is shop. I get in my car thinking I'm going to the library, but I end up at the mall. I shop for recreation, I shop for entertainment. I shop for the heck of it. My new friends tell me, "Let's get together and relax Saturday. We'll meet you at ShopRite." Is this normal?

— Signed Mall Woman

Dear Mall Woman,

Congratulations. You've made a quick adjustment to Orange County life. Paris has its Eiffel Tower, New York City its museums, London its Big Ben. Welcome to Orange County — the land of the low sales tax. Meet you at the Lloyd's between the color TVs and the sweat socks.

Dr. Lefty Laughingstock knows little but answers all. Send your problems in care of this column. And if you ask me, the German shepherd's concern for protocol shows good breeding. She'll make a great bridesmaid.

Chapter 3:

On Being a Columnist and Editor

"Where I have been for most of the past quarter-century is community journalism. I practice it here at the *Times Herald-Record*, the newspaper I believe in. As I discovered, it is my life's calling."   — Mike Levine, 2003

Welcome Home to Your Paper

A funny thing happened to me on the way to writing my next column. I became the editor of the newspaper. If you wonder where I've been the past couple weeks, I've been getting my head examined.

Column writing is the plum job in journalism. You make your living opening your big trap. If you get people angry or make them laugh, you get immediate reaction. You can stand up for the hardworking stiff, hail the everyday heroes and tell the bullies where to get off.

Why in God's creation would I want to be a newspaper editor? Nothing but headaches. Planning meetings, wow, that's a lot of laughs. You work through other people and your imprint often isn't seen for months.

But I've come to see that this community and this newspaper need each other. Sometimes it seems we have lost touch. I burn to help us connect again.

You know, with this new millennium jazz, the newspaper industry is full of all sorts of trendy techno-theories. We're information sorters, retrieval specialists, data analysts. Blah, blah, blah.

Sue me, but I imagine a community journalist as an old-fashioned town doctor or teacher. Not that we can repair a broken arm or unlock the secrets of algebra. But we play an intimate, vital role in the life of a community.

We must be reliable. We must tell people's stories with dignity, honor the heroes among us, defend a community's interests. We must chronicle births and passings, triumphs and sorrows as the important events they are. If we sometimes hold up a mirror that reveals warts, it is only to ask if change is necessary.

And because we live here, we must ply our trade not just with skill, but with heart.

The best community journalists at this newspaper have been strong enough to weep at the murder of a child. They've missed a great news photo to jump into a river to save a stranded soul. They've gone through hell and back to come up with the news your government wanted to keep from you.

I hear nonsense that people don't need community newspapers anymore. They're needed more than ever. In a brave new world that dissects us into consumers and market segments and assorted strangers, we need a place to call home.

Welcome home.

We're not a perfect newspaper and we know we must improve. We know that changes aren't made overnight and we think you know that, too. But we do some fine work here. We're bursting to do more.

Your loyal readership is a way of keeping faith as we grow closer to you. Please send in your questions and comments and, each week, we'll talk in this column.

As a columnist, I was paid to have opinions. As the editor, it's my job to make certain this newspaper is fair and accurate. But I must tell you we will have our bedrock beliefs. When it comes to fighting for justice, when it comes to standing up for the people of our communities, when it comes to giving voice to the hard-working and worn and forgotten, we will be there.

Call us with your stories. Tell us how we can better be your daily companion. We're a newspaper. And every morning, we make house calls.

Nine Years Has Caused Real Change

March 22, 1992

This week, I begin my 10th year of writing this column. I know this doesn't exactly rank with the Bicentennial or even National Yo-Yo Week. But because this is the best job in America, I feel like celebrating.

Through your loyalty, you have given me a livelihood. Through your kindness and honesty, you have changed me.

Sure, in some ways, I'm the same loud mouth that started yapping nine years ago. But this is a humbling business. I've learned a thing or two from you.

This is a good time to remind myself of them so I won't forget.

Be tolerant of other people's opinions.

I don't know how many letters I get that start out something like, "I don't often agree with your views but I enjoy reading your column."

That sets a standard of respect and tolerance I've learned to follow in my column. It's fine to be furious at the actions of a public official, but it can never be a personal attack. I'm a guy giving an opinion, not God pronouncing judgment.

I've also learned there is no shame in apologizing when I mess up. Understand what real courage is all about.

Some columnists fancy that they are courageous. Nonsense. It's our job to shoot our mouths off.

But some of you risk your jobs to speak up for your beliefs.

Profound courage surrounds us. I've met brave whistleblowers, daring firefighters, determined single mothers. I've seen powerless people stand up to bullies and businesspeople with lots to lose do the right thing, anyway.

Dignity lives inside the most humble of us.

I can't believe the knocks some people take. They lose loved ones, life savings, jobs, homes. What's incredible is their resilience. People carry their burdens with amazing grace.

Most people try to do the right thing.

You know, you can explain the greed in the world. You can account for brutishness. But how do you explain the goodness? I've met so many people who lead with their hearts. From the people I've met through this column, I discovered that along with courage, giving is the key to happiness.

Anyone can give at any time. After the rabbi emeritus of my temple died last week, a local nurse called me. She was with the rabbi in his final days. She said he died with such dignity, it was inspiring. Not being Jewish, she wondered if it would be all right to come to the memorial service for him.

Really, this column has made me become an optimist about the human race. Maybe we're not perfect, but we try hard.

The greatest lie is stereotyping.

During our boom and our bust, it was easy to pigeonhole people. This job taught me the foolishness of it. You get up close to anyone and stereotypes fall apart.

There's no such thing as a hunter type or a city type or a racial type. I've met only thousands of very different people, most of whom are united by a common purpose — to lead useful lives surrounded by loved ones.

Because of this column, I've made real friends with people who I never would have met otherwise. Farmers and professors and even a former politician or two. I think I write less about types and more about people.

My job is to start the conversation, not end it.

The reader must always get the last word. I do not publicly answer Letters to the Editor because I already had my say.

My biggest regret is that the volume of mail and phone calls is sometimes so large, I fall behind. Believe me, I read each one carefully. Each one deserves a reply.

For a columnist could not have better readers.

I have proof. One lovely reader even agreed to marry me. We have two children who we love more than life itself.

Maybe that's why I feel as fresh and impassioned as the first day I wrote. There's work to be done, issues to be tackled, a better world to make.

Thank you for allowing me to continue to put in my two cents.

City Boy Sees Country, Likes It and Stays

July 15, 1990

The city boy began his journey on an airless "A" train, creaking downtown from Washington Heights. He held one hand to an overhead strap, another to the Daily News. The July swelter wilted his only suit, a gray wool affair reserved for weddings, funerals and job interviews.

At 42nd Street, he double-timed it to Port Authority. He hurried past Greyhound, Trailways, Jersey Transit, past the homeless looking for breakfast money. Where was this outfit called ShortLine?

He climbed on the bus clutching a ticket and a crumpled want ad, his face sweating beads of city soot. Soon, the big bus barreled under the Lincoln Tunnel into the soupy Jersey morning.

After an hour, the sky became brighter, the horizon wider.

The bus passed highway signs marked Monroe, Oxford Depot, Chester.

Farmhouses appeared, with cows on a hillside.

A horse stood in the sun near a barn.

Where the hell am I, wondered the city boy, Wyoming? How can I even think of coming up here?

It was a funny notion at that. He had lived in New York City his entire 28 years. He walked city, he talked city, he still played schoolyard stickball. His idea of "way upstate" was Yonkers.

The bus rolled along the highway. He passed more signs — Florida, Goshen. Where is this? Never should've even applied here. Thank goodness the job interview the day before in Boston had gone well.

He pulled a soggy road map out of his inside suit pocket. He quickly glanced over the names in the smallest print. Otisville, Hurleyville, Marlboro, Coldenham, Pine Bush. Never heard of 'em, meant nothing at all. Might as well be in Tibet.

The bus turned into the City of Middletown. A city they call this? It looked like a gray railroad town of narrow, crooked, seemingly deserted streets. The railroad must have left town a long time ago, the city boy figured. Well, you know what New Yorkers say, he told himself. When you're out of town, you're out of town.

He took a cab to the job interview. He stayed there a few hours. It sounded like a good career opportunity.

Maybe he could just live here for a short while and move on. He didn't have to be a part of this area. It wasn't like he was going to plant roots here.

He walked back toward the Middletown bus station. He stopped at a luncheonette. When he heard a group of diners laugh at an inside joke, the city boy felt lonely.

He stopped at a stationery store and bought a pack of gum. Hello, a woman said warmly to the city boy.

Hello? Who says hello when you buy gum? He had to admit he was glad she did.

When he got home, he found that the Boston job had come through. At least that was a real city. He expected to tell them yes.

He was surprised when he took the job offer in Middletown.

Exactly 10 years to the day have passed since the city boy took the bus trip to the mid-Hudson.

I'm glad I came.

The job worked out great. I met my wife here and I cannot imagine life without her or without our children.

It's even more than that. Each highway sign that once meant nothing to me now teems with vital connections. The little towns on the map are filled with memories of remarkable people, good times, funerals, flat tires, laughter, friends, tragedies and rebirths.

The woman who sold me the gum became the subject for my first newspaper story here. She introduced me to some of her customers. They had stories, too. I told them some of mine. Friendships were born.

This is how it is for us immigrants. At first, we are so very lost. Then someone says hello. One thing leads to another.

One day we discover this is home.

What I Learned From You

September 14, 2001

Dear friends,

This week is lousy with terrible farewells so I was planning to slip out quietly. Folks have more important matters to consider than one guy changing jobs. But after 21 years, I can't walk away without saying goodbye.

Consider this a letter, not a column, a whisper instead of a speech. I don't want anything to get in our way here. I owe you the truth.

A generation ago, I stepped off a ShortLine bus in Middletown. I saw an old railroad city without a railroad. I heard the sour laughter of old men who knew better times. I saw women who seemed to be everyone's mother and nobody's wife. I found good people working honest and hard. It was a boiling, gray July morning and as I shuffled toward the newspaper office, I heard a rustling breeze and I felt the hand of God.

This is where I was supposed to be.

Dead broke, I stayed in a welfare hotel in Goshen. I had no car. By foot and hitchhike and bus, I set off to listen to people's stories and the stories lifted me beyond my talents.

I wasn't a natural writer. I just kept my eyes and ears open. Then I wrestled with your stories until I discovered the holiness in them.

I learned that humble people can do extraordinary things. The most damaged person has enormous resilience. The most flawed soul can rise up at any minute and help save the world. And I learned that people don't need things — we need each other. We crave community.

Years passed. No matter how rocky my life got, your stories kept me grounded. Over time, I stumbled upon some small accolades in the journalism world but I always knew my column here was what I was meant to do.

Not that I was all that good at it sometimes. I'm glad I picked fights with powerful blowhards. I've been a blowhard myself at times. Stupid, callous words I've written still make me wince. I learned how to apologize.

As years went on, I took on more responsibility at a paper I love. You must understand. This is a special newspaper. Lord knows, we have our flaws but we also have guts, passion, a watchdog's growl, a neighbor's good heart and a true love for our communities.

So when this newspaper called my name to serve as editor, I answered. I'm glad I did. Thanks to the dedicated people here, we're doing some great work. I'm so proud of my colleagues.

But the administrative demands of the job meant I could no longer tell stories. I couldn't hear God anymore.

Each of us has something that connects us to ourselves and our Creator. For me, it's telling people's stories.

And so I must take my leave. It's odd. After all the battles, after all the shouting and laughter and anger, all I am left with today is an enormous sense of gratitude.

For you, for my colleagues, for every moment of the past 21 years. No man could be more privileged.

With my exquisite sense of timing, I take a job in the war zone of Manhattan. Part of the job includes traveling by airplane. Good move, Levine.

I wish we could laugh. There is no conversation that does not bring us back to the evil of this week. I say goodbye to you in a world that needs to know we need community more than ever. Please stay together. I remain your neighbor.

And if anyone ever needs testimony about the everyday goodness in the world, I will tell them about you. About your enormous kindnesses to others and to me. I hope my stories have stood as testimony to your holiness.

Chapter 4:

Mike as Watchdog

"We must have a strong free press in an area with few media outlets. If we don't do the tough story, no one else will."
— Mike Levine, 2003

Tangled Web Only the State Can Perceive

November 28, 1984

Welcome, ladies and gentlemen, to another episode of Great Moments in Bureaucracy. We're brought to you this week by the state of New York, the nation's leading manufacturer of red tape, guaranteed to gum up your lives or your forms back.

This week's unlucky guest star is Richardine Pena of Liberty. Richardine is a 29-year-old waitress, taxpayer, solid citizen. In other words, she's just the type the bureaucracy loves to tangle in its web.

Her story begins in September 1983, when Richardine went to an auction conducted by Sullivan County. Among the items being auctioned was a 1979 Ford LTD, previously belonging to the Sullivan County District Attorney's Office. She bid $550, paid up and the car was hers.

Like most unsuspecting citizens, Richardine believed this was a simple transaction. You give them the money, file the papers, insure the car and drive away.

But not so fast. She was told that the title to the car was temporarily unavailable. She shouldn't worry, though. Everything would be straightened out pronto.

Sure.

Because Richardine Pena could not keep an unregistered car on the street, much less drive it, she had to put it in storage.

Meanwhile, the DA's office, unable to locate the title, wrote to Motor Vehicle in Albany for another copy. Writing to the state of New York is like sending a message to a black hole in space. Nothing comes back.

Richardine keeps calling the DA's office. Every time she hears the same reply — we're working on it.

Well, apparently, they were. Motor Vehicle finally writes back the DA's office saying they have no record of the title anywhere. Ah, c'mon, says the DA's office, we drove it for four years, registered and insured. There has to be a title.

Uh-uh, says Motor Vehicle. There's no title. And if there's no title, announced the state of New York, this car hereby does not exist.

That the car never existed would have come as a great comfort to Richardine Pena at that point, if only she weren't being billed for storage on it.

Meanwhile, seasons pass; autumn folds to winter, winter opens to spring, spring blooms to summer. Super Bowls are won and lost, romances blossom and wilt, babies are conceived and born, and Richardine Pena still waits for the title to her 1979 Ford LTD.

Finally, in July, Richardine calls the man who was in charge of the auction, County Commissioner of Public Works Chuck Myers. Look, she says, I spent $550 on this car last September, I still can't drive it, and it's costing me a fortune in storage. Help.

Myers talks to the DA's office and they call in the local Motor Vehicle office to see if they can cut the red tape. But Albany tells them the guy who's in charge of non-existent cards is out. When will he be back? Oh, in a few months, they say. He's on a leave of absence.

To keep a horror story short, the title now exists. Not that Richardine Pena has it. By this time, lawyers are involved, and there's a fight on over storage costs and depreciation. She won't get the title until everything is resolved. Which might be in time for the turn of the century.

But let it never be said that Richardine Pena didn't get anything from this. Fourteen months after buying the untitled DA's car for $550 at the county auction, she now has been billed for storage to the tune of $3,020.

She's also had to go out and buy another car in the meantime. That's cost her an additional $1,200.

"I learned a good lesson," says Richardine, now a year older and wiser. "You can't trust the government to get anything straight."

Well said, Richardine, and with that we conclude this latest episode of Great Moments in Bureaucracy. And remember, in the state of New York, red tape goes in before the name goes on.

Newburgh Election Just Like Mississippi 1965

November 6, 1991

In any other season, it would have been another empty storefront on Broadway. But this was election time, when Newburgh twitches long enough to remind itself why it is in such dire straits.

And so, on one of these storefronts, a faded blue poster urging "Audrey Carey for Mayor" hung on the front window. Inside, campaign manager Rudy LaMarr paced up and down past the bags of doughnuts and coffee.

When the news came in Monday afternoon, LaMarr allowed himself a moment when he thought it might all work out. A state Supreme Court had tossed out 2,000 voting registration challenges made by Republican and Conservative leaders. The idea was to scare away a large turnout among black voters for Audrey Carey.

"They won't have the guts to show up and challenge people one by one," predicted LaMarr.

He was wrong. Newburgh behaved in yesterday's election as if it were Mississippi 1965.

Alison Bethel, a Times Herald-Record reporter and Montgomery Street resident, stopped to vote at the Horizons-on-Hudson School before work.

She walked into the polling place to see uniformed guards. She gave her name and suddenly she heard two women say accusingly, "She's challenged. She's challenged." It was a like a chant.

Alison Bethel is black. The women, both white, pulled Bethel to a side and told her she had to sign papers swearing she lived in the city. Bethel offered to show identification, but she was turned down.

A tall white man yelled out, "She can go to jail if she's lying."

What's going on? Bethel asked.

"Honey," said an elderly woman, "they're trying to stop you from voting, just like they did when I was young."

After 15 rowdy minutes, Bethel was finally allowed to vote. "I'm not easily intimidated," she said, "but this was intimidating. I didn't want to vote after that."

Which was essentially the purpose. Voters, mostly black, were challenged all day long by white politicians. The reign of chaos and fear never sets on this town.

By nightfall, it seemed certain the returns would lag long after the polls closed. There would be the usual charges of foul, counter-foul, calls for impounding the election machines.

At Carey headquarters, they settled in for a long night.

This should have been Audrey Carey's night of early and certain celebration.

She is the Democrat candidate in a town where there are 1,300 more registered Democrats than Republicans.

Audrey Carey has twice lost a race for mayor to white Republicans.

This year, Carey won the Democratic primary. Because her Republican opponent is also black, this suddenly meant there weren't enough candidates in the race.

Two white candidates also showed up to run.

Independent Nick Valentine ran as a nice guy with no experience. Regina D'Angelo, the loser to Carey in the Democratic primary, was a sour grapes entry. She ran on the ironically named Spirit of Newburgh line.

Republican Tyrone Crabb ran as the only black person in Newburgh who doesn't believe race is any sort of problem in this town.

There is no reason to believe any of the candidates are racist. Decisions based on race are simply a reality of Newburgh, as much a part of everyday life as it is in Johannesburg.

Whites live in one part of town, blacks in another. Whites get one level of city services, blacks get a lower level. Most whites are middle class; most blacks are poor.

Most whites vote for whites; most blacks vote for blacks. The council is elected in an at-large system, a sham dismissed by courts as being inherently discriminatory against minorities.

This is how Election Day shaped up. If 70 percent of the registered blacks showed up to vote, Audrey Carey would win. She could expect no more than 5 percent of the vote in white wards.

This is not a damning of the people of Newburgh.

It boasts a school system that has hurdled the race issue better than any in America. Newburgh schools are recognized as among the best in the state.

Municipal leadership has been something else.

Since factories started leaving town 25 years ago, Newburgh politicians have refused to deal with the real issues of jobs and housing and drugs. The problems run so deep, Newburgh became the poorest city in New York.

City leaders couldn't solve those problems so they started pointing fingers. They divided this town over the phony issue of race.

Yesterday, another election was over, but fear and chaos still run through Newburgh. The long night of this river city seemed like it would never end.

The campaign lights will go out and the storefronts will, once again, be empty.

This Padding We Don't Need

Sit down for this one. All curled up in a nice comfy chair paid for by the taxpayers? No?

Then you're living wrong. Should have taken up politics, chump. The chairman of the Orange County Legislature has just redecorated her own office at your expense.

Perhaps this is in honor of the Legislature's recent decision to raise the county sales tax. Roberta Murphy shopped till she dropped our money.

The chairwoman put the touch on us for a dozen chairs at $250 apiece. Upholstered, upscale and uptown. Those are bleacher seats compared to the $485 personal throne the chairman ordered for herself.

Accessories? Murphy also charged us $200 for her own paper shredder. Sure to inspire public confidence in the most secretive public body since the old Soviet Politburo.

Wait, keep your wallet open. You also must pay for new carpeting for the entire Legislature. The carpeting comes to almost $5,000.

Amazing. This is Murphy's Law at work: If there's anything that can be done to rub taxpayers the wrong way, our chairman will do it.

Every political body in the U.S.A. has gotten the message. The party's over. No more fancy decorations, no more secret chambers, no more running up the tab.

But at the Orange County Legislature, the fun's only just begun. In fact, tomorrow night, the Legislature will vote on whether to turn Orange County into a banana republic.

That's right. The Legislature will decide whether you, the taxpayer, have a right to speak at County Legislature meetings. A motion to bar the public from speaking has already passed committee.

Legislator Dino Sciamanna says he's had it with having to listen to you yahoos who pay his salary. He storms out when the public speaks. Last meeting, he told fellow legislators, "I don't have to listen to this garbage."

Like when the Legislature passed the new budget, a few members of the public wanted their say. The agenda said they could. But Murphy pulled a fast one and passed the budget before the public was allowed to speak.

This got a few taxpayers hot under the collar. So Murphy decided to get sheriff's deputies to protect the Legislature from us rabble. Even if they have to yank deputies off patrol.

The question is, who's going to protect us from the Legislature?

At the same time the Legislature will hit us up for a tax increase, they have kept in the budget a $10,000 slush fund for legislative travel. Last year, Murphy and Co. spent it on a trip to Las Vegas. Saw Gladys Knight and the Pips on your nickel. I heard it through the grapevine and I saw it on the expense line.

The grapevine also carries the Legislature's next redecorating effort.

They're putting out bids for new chairs to refurbish the Republican caucus room. That's the caucus room the Legislature does public business in and to which the public is not invited. I know. I got tossed out of there last year trying to cover public business.

I guess I was sitting on their chairs too hard.

They want new ones. The county is putting out a bid for 30 mid-backed upholstered armed swivel tilt chairs. They expect it to cost about $250 a pop, so that comes to another $7,500.

I have a better idea. Folding chairs. Our legislators should sit on simple folding chairs. It may remind them that they are hired hands.

Their bosses are the hard-pressed people of Orange County, most of whom have never spent $250 for a chair in their lives.

I called Elliott's office furniture in Middletown. A folding chair is $10.60 apiece. Problem solved.

Call me a softie, but I believe rank has its privileges. Chairman Roberta deserves a folding chair with padding. That's $16 even.

OK, for 30 chairs and one padded one, it's $323.49, delivery included. Of course, that's not including county sales tax. A tax, which you shall soon notice, is on its way up in the banana republic of Orange.

Make Them Write Clearly

I can't do my job anymore.

The boss says I'm supposed to look at public affairs and throw in my two cents. The problem is, I don't understand a word anyone is saying.

I just got my hands on a report from the Pine Bush School District on early education. It might be brilliant. I haven't the slightest idea what it says.

Go ahead. You try your luck at it:

"By not providing experiences that enhance the development of all domains, a child's interaction with his/her total environment will be altered."

We must incorporate "whole language activities" and "move away from psychometric measures which are limited to a multiple-choice selection."

And, as everyone knows, we must "encourage schools to integrate hands-on learning, conceptual learning that leads to understanding along with acquisition of basic skills, meaningful learning experiences, interactive teaching and cooperative learning into a broad range of relevant content."

What in the world are they talking about? I don't understand Gobbledygook, the official language of public affairs that's spreading like fertilizer.

I have to read stuff from state Social Services that talks about "inter-dependent support networks for needs assessment of children at risk." Say what?

As for Pentagon briefings, why don't they just do them in Pig Latin? They can't call a smoke bomb a smoke bomb. It's a "universal obscurant."

I have a modest proposal. Anything paid for by the taxpayer must be understandable to the average taxpayer. Otherwise, we don't pay for it.

That means all tax increases must hereby be labeled as just that. If it's called "revenue enhancement" or "user fees," we ain't paying.

All government functions must be fewer than five syllables. We now have an agency called "Federal Insurance Administration, Office of Risk Assessment, Technical Operations Division, Production Control Branch of the Federal Emergency Management Agency."

Four people work there. If they can't explain what they do more clearly, zap 'em off the taxpayer payroll.

Bombs and bullets must be called what they are. If the Pentagon calls them "consumables" or "radiation enhancement weapons," we ain't paying for them.

Anyone who applies for a government grant better talk plain English. No more taxpayer money for "implementing an evaluation program to address situation parameters in exurban environments."

Why do people speak Gobbledygook?

The most innocent reason is that some smart people mistakenly believe it makes them sound smarter.

It gets more sinister. For some, Gobbledygook covers up the fact they don't know what they're talking about.

Or maybe if they're vague, they feel they won't be held accountable. Don't hold a teacher responsible for teaching your child. Because she's not a teacher. She's a "classroom manager" or "learning facilitator."

Then we have the political reasons for Gobbledygook.

Nobody wants to say what's really going on.

The Florida State Legislature has banished the word "remedial" from any mention. It doesn't look good.

From here on, declares the Legislature, "remedial courses" must be called "college preparatory instruction."

See, already Florida is doing a better job. It now has nobody in need of "remedial" courses. In fact, everyone's getting ready for college.

"No, ma'am, don't say your 12-year-old child can't read. He simply has yet to master the whole phonic experience in his college preparatory instructions."

The first step in improving government and education is to force everyone to speak clearly.

It's for everyone's own good. Underneath all the Pine Bush Gobbledygook, I sense a genuine passion for helping kids.

But when the Pine Bush report says, "We must also look at the issues of assessment of program outcomes," nobody knows it's talking about accountability.

So here's the first rule in accountability to the taxpayers: What we don't understand, we don't pay for.

Can't say it any plainer than that.

Discounting the Premium on Pretty

Deep in a shopping mall, Miss Middletown of 1944 inhales a Virginia Slims menthol and, just as effortlessly, exhales a stream of polished conversation.

"This is such a wonderful experience for the girls," says the gracious Betty Drennan. "It's something they'll never forget."

She surveys a gaggle of nervous teenage girls before her. "Is this your first time as a judge?"

It is, I tell Mrs. Drennan. Out of respect for her enthusiasm, I do not tell her that I dislike beauty contests. I agreed to be a judge in the Miss Teen Orange County contest because I've never said no to a public invitation.

And so Mrs. Drennan and I, along with insurance salesman Steve Zakrewski, are led to the judges' table. One by one, the 32 girls are led before us for a "personality" interview. Two and a half minutes for each girl. Rate them on a scale of 1 to 30. Mrs. Drennan gently asks their ages and interests. Some girls' faces tremble with fright.

I ask each one why they are here.

For the experience, they say. Some have already begun a modeling career and a high pageant finish looks great on the resume. The winner also goes to the state teen pageant. This is serious business for them — for some, a modeling career is their only ticket out of the ordinary life.

"I want to travel to Europe," says one, eagerly. "To Paris, to everywhere."

"Interesting," Mrs. Drennan tells her through a frosty smile. "I've been in Middletown all my life and I've never had the urge to travel anywhere."

Other girls say they are here because they want to see what it's like. Some want to be doctors, dentists, chemical engineers, psychologists. One is a volunteer on a crisis hot line. They're proud they had the nerve to try something different, to take center stage. "It's the kind of thing you can tell your kids about," says one.

The personality "test" is over. "They're so lovely and bright and poised," says Mrs. Drennan, happy that these traits have survived these 40 years of history. Indeed, these girls are very nice people.

Five hours later, these very nice people are on stage in bathing suits before a large crowd. Some contestants are 13 years old. It's just not right; 13-year-old girls should not have their figures judged, except maybe by 13-year-old boys.

"I felt so embarrassed," says one of the girls afterwards. So did I.

The next morning, I call Rose Capozella, the Orange County pageant director. "Listen," she says. "It's a part of the universe. There are all sorts of pageants — for muscles, for brains, whatever. This one's for beauty. There's nothing wrong with that."

That night, I tell Betty Drennan of my reservations about the beauty pageants. She answers with conviction: "This is a way for these girls to better their lives," she says. "That takes courage."

The crowd huddles in the mall for the finals. "These girls got their noses stuck in the air," announces a teenage boy in a ratty T-shirt. He whistles and hoots.

The girls, wearing evening gowns, are escorted onstage by Marines. In judging, I lean toward kindness of face and grace of manner. But who am I to assign a point total to a face?

The semi-finalists give a one-minute speech. The winner has the highest combined point total from the three judges of all events. She is Stacey Saltzberg of Middletown, who seems like a lovely person. They all do. Picking winners is as arbitrary as good looks.

Betty Drennan, Miss Middletown of 1944, extends her hand and tells us how wonderful it's been. The girls embrace each other. Any disappointment is hidden with a grace unmatched by at least a few parents.

I leave them, still no fan of beauty contests, but an admirer of 32 girls who rose above nerves and catcalls, in pursuit of a better life.

Forty years ago, beauty contests were one of the only tickets to center stage. The next morning's headlines about a woman on another kind of ticket, suggest the daughters of these girls may be able to bypass the swimsuit contest on their way to the presidency.

More Phony Baloney From a Meat Market

Here come the sex police. This time, they're after Miss Ulster County, Jennifer Delora of Stone Ridge.

Well, she used to be Miss Ulster County. The New York State Pageant lifted her crown last week.

Jennifer Delora is an actress, having appeared on two network TV shows. Before becoming Miss Ulster County, she had the starring role in an R-rated horror film. There was a 10-second shower scene in the movie.

Like most people who take showers, Jennifer Delora took her clothes off. She was shown briefly on camera from the rib cage up.

The film went nowhere, never even making it into a major theatrical release.

End of story.

Hot stuff, huh? The only people the film managed to excite were the beauty pageant operators.

Joan Jones of Watertown is executive director of the New York State Beauty Pageant. This is what she had to say, after the very important board of directors took away Jennifer Delora's crown:

"I don't know what could be more indecent or in bad taste."

Well, Joan, maybe we can help you out.

For starters, there's that grubby meat market you run called a beauty pageant. Let's fess up, Joan, you don't put the contestants in swimsuits to show off their brains. Take away the flesh parade and you're out of business.

So it's only fair to say you profit from the display of women's bodies.

Let's see, what else can be more indecent than a woman being photographed while taking a shower?

How 'bout humiliating her in public about it? That's what you did, Joan. You got some anonymous calls about a film that was never even released in movie theaters, a film the public never even saw or cared about.

But you had to go make a big deal about it, flogging Jennifer Delora in public as if she had committed a crime. Her parents had seen the film and they weren't offended. What offended them was your organization branding their daughter as a moral leper.

Let me ask you something, ma'am. What if you had a chance to have your five-and-dime pageant hosted by Julie Andrews or Meryl Streep or Sally Fields?

It seems to me you'd jump at the chance to be associated with such well-respected actresses and Academy Award winners.

Betcha it wouldn't matter to you that all three have at one time appeared nude in movies. Betcha you wouldn't have told them "there is nothing more indecent."

Jennifer Delora may not be famous, but she is an actress. She is not a porn star.

She has appeared on the network soap opera "One Life To Live" and the prime-time comedy "Kate and Allie." Her brief appearance in the shower scene was part of a starring role in a horror film.

What would you have her do? Tell the director she's going to keep her clothes on in the shower?

Listen, it's a free country, Joan Jones, and it's your meat market. Do with it what you want. But, just one more thing. You said Jennifer broke her contract that had her promise she never did anything immoral.

Go ahead. Tell us what's immoral about what she did. Tell us who she hurt by her actions. Tell us what law she broke.

In a world filled with obscenities such as starvation, disease and terrorism, it's interesting to know there is "nothing more indecent" to you than a woman being photographed in a shower.

It must be some world you live in, Joan Jones. But what else can we expect from an operation that thinks it can judge morality as easily as it judges the flesh it peddles?

This Flick Rates Just One Garbage Can

Congratulations! You're a movie producer.

You didn't know that? Maybe you missed Tuesday's paper. A legislative commission spent $10,000 making a movie about garbage in New York.

Guess who that $10,000 comes from? That's right, the taxpayer. This bankrolling makes us all movie producers.

Glamour City.

I decided to high-tail it up to Albany to catch the world premiere Tuesday night. I figured I'd report back to my fellow producers on how our investment shapes up. I'm no film or garbage expert, but as creator of the Skunky awards, I do have a working knowledge of performances in smelly terrains.

The picture — "The Mountain In The City" — introduces that budding movie star, Ulster County Assemblyman Maurice "Hollywood" Hinchey. It's about solid waste management in New York.

What's that you say? No one cares about a movie on garbage? Nonsense. The Republicans care.

In fact, they're furious that Waste Commission Chairman Hinchey introduced only Democrats in the picture. They grumble that Democrat Hinchey is looking to run for lieutenant governor. The movie, they say, is a chance to strut his stuff at taxpayer expense.

Aw, c'mon. Who can imagine a politician trying to build his future on a film about garbage? Who would even try?

At the world premiere, held in a hearing room, we are all handed publicity pamphlets.

"The Mountain In The City," it says. Then, right underneath in big bold letters, it trumpets:

"featuring ASSEMBLYMAN MAURICE D. HINCHEY."

On page two, there's a half-page biography of "HOST/ COMMENTATOR, Democrat MAURICE D. HINCHEY." Just a brief sketch, mentioning everything the man has done since 1945.

Page three is filled entirely with two large pictures. Both are portraits of Assemblyman Maurice D. Hinchey.

The caption says "...Maurice D. Hinchey seems equally at home in his office or in front of a camera..."

Attached to the publicity packet is a newsletter from the State Solid Waste Commission, Assemblyman Maurice D. Hinchey, chairman. On the front page is, of all things, a photo of Assemblyman Maurice D. Hinchey.

As screening time nears, the crowd buzzes with excitement. This cavernous modern room, which looks like a courtroom in a Siberian work camp, hushes as a man in a paisley tie steps forward to welcome them.

The man is Assemblyman Maurice D. Hinchey.

He says the film is a group effort.

Then the lights dim and the film begins.

The less said about the movie the better. It is without a doubt the longest hour in the history of mankind. They should donate it to state prisons, its screening used as a threat to keep inmates in line.

Of course, the highlight of the film is Assemblyman Maurice D. Hinchey. He stands on top of Staten Island's Mount Trashmore in work shirt and jeans, his hair waving in the dirty wind. He walks toward the camera saying something indistinguishable about garbage. Definitely lieutenant governor timber.

Assemblyman Maurice D. Hinchey is then upstaged by a shot of six street sweeping machines performing a ballet.

The review in the Albany paper says the movie's pacing is "like an industrial film." The movie's creators say they are going to enter it in film festivals.

My fellow movie producers, I don't think we're going to make our money back on this one. I don't even believe it's going to move anyone to enlist in the fight against garbage.

But maybe, just maybe, we taxpayers have started a movie career for Ulster County Assemblyman Maurice "Hollywood" Hinchey.

I hope so. Nothing in the film suggests a future in politics.

Leaks May Hurt Politicians, But They Help Us

August 9, 1992

A politician's fury over leaked documents was among the 101 things that didn't matter during this past week of blood and sorrow.

But, somehow, that fury connected to the lessons of this tragedy.

The angry politician was Orange County Legislator Roberta Murphy. For those unfamiliar with the feisty Murphy, she does a world-class slow burn. She also packs a great "bang, zoom, to-the-moon-Alice" temper.

This time, Murphy blew up because I obtained some Republican Party files that recently fired Commissioner Shirley Harvey-Cook stored in her county office.

The files showed how party politics invades county government.

What was I to do with these documents?

As a reporter, my job is to get information to the people, who happen to own the government. If ever there was a public issue — party politics in government — this was it.

Excerpts from those files appeared in last Sunday's newspaper.

Murphy went ballistic.

She demanded that the county Legislature launch an investigation — at taxpayer expense — to find out where I got these documents. She would like the district attorney to get involved.

They should all save their breath and get on with the business of running a county. It will be a cold day in hell before a reporter reveals his sources.

But Murphy's outburst and the events of last week raise a more important question.

Who owns information gathered by public officials and stored in public buildings?

The press says it's the people's.

The government says it knows best what information the people are entitled to.

Some of this information is ridiculous, like the Republican Party declarations of "war" stored in Cook's office.

Some of it is critical.

All of it should be public.

Last week, Middletown's mayor and police chief chose not to alert the public even though they knew a serial killer might be on the loose.

The rationale, that they didn't want to panic women or alert the killer, is absurd.

What did they want to do, lure the killer by using the women of Middletown as bait?

If I'm a woman or the parent of a girl, I have a right to know if the city believes a serial killer may be on the loose. I'll decide whether or not I want to panic.

Government does not own the information. We hire them to be our servants.

It's time to remind government of that. But, first, government agencies have to remind each other.

In April, the state Parole Board was trying to determine whether to release Nathaniel White, shortly before a series of killings he now says he committed. They heard that White was involved in a child abuse case.

A parole officer called the Orange County Department of Social Services to find out more about the charges against White. DSS told parole to go take a flying leap.

Our reporters found this out by getting information the bureaucracy had kept hidden.

Could these killings have been prevented if public information had been shared and not secreted? Maybe, just maybe they could have. We're having a devil of a time finding out. Some in government are still attempting to hide information, protecting their own fiefdoms.

Certainly, some public information needs to be confidential to protect people's privacy. But, by and large, the public has a right to know what information its own employees have collected. The press has a right to print what it finds out.

Let the people decide what to make of the facts.

What's chilling is that Murphy and Gert Mokotoff, the Middletown mayor, both intelligent people, aren't buying that.

And because the press has become the all-American scapegoat, the government has managed to get many people to take its side.

Lord knows, the press makes mistakes. Lord knows, we sometimes go overboard. We can abuse our rights.

Shame on us for that.

But Thomas Jefferson wasn't stupid. He said if it's a choice between having a free press or a government, go with the free press.

So let government officials understand:

They work for the people. The information officials gather on our behalf belongs not to the government. It belongs to all of us.

Rebel Doctor Puts Others' Health Above His Own Gain

July 18, 1999

Last time Dr. Larry Glass got in trouble was when a drug company sent free clocks to an Orange County Mental Health office. Each clock had the name of a prescription drug printed across its face. The clocks were placed in the therapy offices.

So Glass is doing a session when the client looks at the clock and says she was once prescribed the drug and it stunk. Another client looks at the clock and says he's taking that drug. How much does it cost you, asks Glass?

Client says 60 tablets cost $300 a month.

That's enough for Glass. He's not going to some la-de-da meeting and discuss it. Up against the wall, drug companies.

Springing into his takin'-it-to-the-streets mode, Glass goes around to each of the therapist's offices and removes the clocks.

This, he says, gets fellow staffers nuts. Glass is told he needs counseling for invading personal space and other platitudes. He apologizes if anyone got bent out of shape, but...

"I look to stir the pot," says Larry Glass, gonzo psychiatrist, MD.

Beautiful. In an age and a county known for its go-along-to-get-along ways, Larry Glass is an endangered species — a rebel.

He looks like Jerry Garcia. His patients liken him to Patch Adams. Some of his colleagues liken him to a pain in the butt.

With only three years to go to get his 20 years in as a state psychiatrist, Glass up and quit Mid-Hudson Psych. "A matter of integrity," he says. Long story.

Then Glass left a local not-for-profit because he felt they were running a money mill and damn the clients. He yells at psychiatrists who turn away patients who can't pay. He rails against pill-pushing practices that live on prescription pads.

"You can't treat people as objects," he says. "You need to take the time to really listen to them."

Glass runs a weekly phobic disorder group in Orange County, made up of people who suffer paralyzing panic attacks. Patients call him day and night. He makes house calls. He charges group members nothing.

"It's more important people get better than I get rich," he says, about to get himself kicked out of the '90s.

I raise the name of Larry Glass because there's damn few rebels around, anymore.

The message these days is don't rock the boat, be with the team, act nice, stay scared, keep dancing for the money. And, most of all, keep our mouths shut in the face of injustice. Get real, we have possessions to protect.

We need to remind each other there's a different way. We can take a stand and live. As our region sinks into suburban conformity, let us now praise the rebels amongst us.

Know anyone who bucks the system to make the world better? Let me know. We can celebrate them here.

Sure, rebels can rub people the wrong way. They can be contrary, annoying, deadly righteous, even dead wrong. And one more thing.

All progress depends on them.

Glass left the mental health center a few weeks ago. But before he left, two staffers took apart the clocks and blotted over the name of the advertised drug with pictures of animals. No more pill-pushing on the face of the clocks.

This is what rebels do. They change the times.

Normal Isn't Always Nice

July 5, 1991

The town supervisor heard about it last Wednesday morning. Word spread: Eight retarded people wanted to move into Arcadia Hills.

By the next evening, 150 Arcadia Hills residents packed a Goshen Town Board meeting. This threat had to be stopped immediately.

"They're dangerous and they steal," one resident said of the eight people he had never met.

"I don't want these people in my neighborhood," shouted another. One after another, alarmed Arcadia Hills residents said they feared for their safety and their children's safety.

Several residents, apparently assuming there is a legal right to vote on who can live next door, screamed, "What about my rights?"

The politicians ate it up. Goshen Supervisor Myron Urbanski assured Arcadia Hills residents that the retarded people would only be allowed to move in over his "dead body." Applause thundered in the roomful of the non-retarded.

You hear this snarl of rage whenever anyone different wants to move onto one of our suburban streets.

In the Land of Normal, they snarl at the lame, the poor and the ill. But especially the retarded.

Last July, eight retarded people moved into a house on Overhill Road in Middletown.

Some of these people had been freed after years in dark, crowded, faceless institutions. The residence gave them an opportunity to go to work, to cook their own meals and to clean their own rooms, small, precious measures of dignity.

The residents had 24-hour supervision, just like there would be in Arcadia Hills.

Some Overhill Road neighbors went nuts. Shortly after the retarded residents moved in to their new home, their windows were pelted with apples and tomatoes.

Last week, on the heels of the Arcadia Hills hysteria, I visited the house on Overhill Road run by Occupations. I thought maybe folks would like to see the "dangerous" lifestyles of the retarded.

Steve Raisman welcomed me. "Let me show you around," he said. And he did. Downstairs, upstairs, through the neatly kept bedrooms, the spotless kitchen, past the exercycle.

The residents had just come home from work. One resident was quietly doing a jigsaw puzzle. Another was working out on the exercycle. A third was watching a TV show.

Some were busy preparing dinner. They all take turns cooking, doing the dishes and going grocery shopping.

Weird place, huh?

I asked Raisman about his life. He is 38 and mentally retarded. He loves '50s music and mystery movies. He plays softball in an Orange County League integrated with retarded and non-retarded players.

I spoke with other residents. Lynn Turner talked about growing up in Port Jervis. Sandi Hill showed me her Special Olympics medals. Margaret Stevens was looking forward to her 60th birthday next Saturday. She had spent much of her life holed up in Letchworth, so this was special.

They all wanted to talk about last week's vacation. They had saved their money and rented cabins at Lake George (cabins that were shared with non-retarded people). They went swimming, boating, even bought a few souvenirs.

How are the neighbors, I asked. "Fine," Ms. Hill said. "They wave to us and they speak to us. They're really nice to us around here."

That's because the residents improve any neighborhood just by showing up. The retarded in group homes have an unbeatable track record. In the four homes and three apartments run by Occupations, no resident has ever been charged with a crime. None. Not even jay-walking.

That doesn't matter to the people in the Land of Normal who know better. They know that being different is a sign of danger.

At the Goshen board meeting last week, one of the Arcadia Hills residents demanded to know if they could get a guarantee no one would be hurt by the retarded people.

Maybe it is the retarded people who should demand the guarantee.

People from the Land of Normal can be dangerous.

The Skunk Meets His Match, Odor-Wise

Once upon a time, the Oscars were America's way of congratulating itself on producing the most popular movie-makers in the world.

This year, though, not one of the five nominees for best director was an American.

OK, so we don't make such terrific cars or toasters, anymore, but movies? What is this country coming to?

That's why it's reassuring to know that somewhere in America, there's a place where this nation is still tops. A place where all the winners are homegrown.

That place is the mid-Hudson and the awards are the Skunkies. The Skunkies reward mid-Hudson institutions and elected officials for the most memorable performances of greed, waste and arrogance. We never have to go to Europe for our winners.

Here's the latest round of Skunkies (no writer's strike here), so sit back, relax and break out the popcorn. Drum roll and envelope, please.

To the Village of Goshen Board of Trustees for worst performance in a governmental role in "Fatal Election."

Marcia Mattheus believed her village of Goshen was growing too big, too fast, too haphazardly. She challenged the entrenched Goshen political establishment by running for a seat on the Village Board. She narrowly lost.

The board responded by kicking her off the village Planning Board. The board also replaced Reynell Andrews, who supported Mrs. Mattheus in the election.

The only board member who opposed this petty vindictiveness was Robert Weinberger. For taking a stand, he was removed as chairman of the village Police Committee.

Some nerve she had in running. What did she think this was, a democracy?

For worst performance in a do-nothing role to Kingston officials led by Mayor Richard White in "White Trash."

For seven years, the city of Kingston has been told its landfill was nearing capacity; the city had better look for alternatives.

For seven years, while Kingston choked in garbage, city officials fiddled. What little they did was much too late. On Monday, the state closed the city's landfill. As of yesterday afternoon, the mayor still had no plan as to where the city was going to put its garbage. Only last night did city officials begin to find a temporary solution.

Here's a Skunky for city officials, if they can smell it above the stench of the landfill.

To the state Department of Transportation for worst road show performance in "The Hole Truth."

The lifeblood of Sullivan County is tourism. The main highway in Sullivan County is Route 17. From Livingston Manor to Parksville, Route 17 resembles the moon. Big, deep craters of potholes all over.

The state Department of Transportation, which seems to always be fixing things in Senate Majority Leader Warren Anderson's Binghamton part of the district, says it doesn't have the money to fix up Sullivan County.

The Skunk has a solution. Taxpayers should buy Warren Anderson a summer home in Sullivan County. That way, he'll have to tiptoe through the potholes on Route 17.

The Department of Transportation might have all the potholes fixed in less than a week.

To Robert Marino for worst performance in a healthful role in "Dumbstruck."

Some folks feel Orange County government is second rate except for its Health Department, which is third rate. Perish the thought. The county has such a good reputation and pays so well that Robert Marino of South Carolina was the only qualified applicant who bothered to seek the health commissioner's post.

How excited was Marino at this prospect?

At first Marino accepted the job offer. Then he changed his mind and said no. Then he reconsidered and said yes. Then he said no again.

Finally, he said yes again and began work Feb. 29.

He quit after one week.

From now on in the mid-Hudson, to keep changing your mind is to pull a Marino.

When he comes back again, he can pick up his Skunky.

Too Young to Qualify for Justice

December 2, 1983

Every other week, the judge says, the mother must send her daughter, Suzy, off for a visit.

Her daughter tells her about these visits. The mother says Suzy told her that on one of these visits she has been put in bed with two men. And that the two men — one of them her father — told Suzy it is all right if they kiss her and touch her because they love her. Following other visits, Suzy tells her mother that her father touched her all over her body.

Suzy is 3 years old.

Child therapists say it is nearly impossible for a 3-year-old to make up stories like this. The mother says Suzy sometimes comes home from these visits unable or unwilling to walk. She clings to her mother. Suzy is now under psychiatric care.

***

The legal system says the mother must continue to send her daughter away even though the little girl tells of being sexually molested. If not, Suzy will be taken away from her mother.

The legal system basically says that as along as a child molester does not leave any marks, he can go on molesting as long as he's given the opportunity.

Because in order to prove guilt, penetration or bruises must be shown. Otherwise, there must be a witness to other forms of molestation.

Being under 6 years old, Suzy cannot testify on her own behalf. A child counts for next to nothing in the legal system.

But Suzy's father has all the right in the world to see her, according to the visitation agreement in her parents' divorce. He suffers no consequences. He doesn't even have to pay for the intensive psychiatric counseling Suzy is now undergoing.

The only thing the legal system has offered on behalf of Suzy is that the mother can hire someone to watch the child while she is visiting her father. The mother finds it difficult to hire people who want to take on that responsibility.

As long as the legal system mandates these visits, the mother wants the court to appoint someone to protect Suzy whenever she is in the presence of her father. The mother says she is not denying the right of the father to visit the child. She said she wants Suzy "to have a father, but I want her to be safe."

To that end, the mother says she is willing to split the cost of this supervision with Suzy's father. It will cost the taxpayer nothing.

"I am angry at my ex-husband but he is a sick man," says the mother. "The justice system is supposed to be well. They're supposed to protect her. But in court the battle is over his rights and my rights. What about my daughter's rights?

"Her rights should be above all others. She is a child. Why are they letting her suffer? Can't somebody help?"

Suzy's mother did manage to hire one person to supervisor the father-daughter's visits. He sat in the living room while Suzy's father gave her a three-hour bath. Her mother says Suzy later told her that Daddy went pee-pee in the bathtub while she was in it.

***

I wish I could tell you this column is about fictional characters. It is not.

These people live in the mid-Hudson. Little else is revealed about their specific whereabouts or other events that might in any way reveal the child's identity. Her name has been changed.

I also wish I could tell you these were certainly the rantings of a mother in a fit of vindictiveness against her ex-husband. But transcripts and conversations with others have convinced me her story is true.

Like other recent columns here about child abuse, this story is told in the hope that our courts will begin to protect our children.

Because judges continue to lecture us about the rights of adults while a 3-year-old is sentenced to a nightmare without end.

How dare they?

Maybe the judges know about the law, but many of them have yet to learn the meaning of justice.

No Happy Returns on 'Psycho Selloff'

February 26, 1984

I'm not one of those anti-hunting zealots, so gun store ads don't normally throw me for a loop. But I was bothered by a big ad in the Times Herald-Record a week or so ago for a gun store in Dutchess County.

"Assault rifles," said one heading listing military weapons that seemed useful only if you wanted to declare war against Connecticut.

"Colt Crazyness," cheered another heading.

And then the ad apparently alerted us to a special sale for John Hinckley and other homicidal lunatics. It listed weapons at discount prices and hailed it as nothing less than a "Psycho Selloff."

As a private business, the Record has the right to run or reject any advertisement or any part of its contents. It regularly rejects ads concerning a person's sexual orientation. But it decided to run this ad.

And there was nary a complaint from readers. A community that has a heart attack over nudity does not even raise its blood pressure about a verbal orgy to psychotic violence.

Because for many people, violence — not sex — is the erotic release.

We salute violence. We respect it. We roll in it.

In that honkytonk affair that the Orange County Fair has become, it was the women's mud wrestling that sold the joint out last year. Professional wrestling regularly packs 'em in all over.

The rising figures on domestic violence suggest that we accept brutality as a release from stress.

And while the area endlessly debates the appearance of the Playboy Channel over private airways, your child will see close to 5,000 murders on commercial TV by the time he is 10. Not one peep about that.

Maybe only the sickest of the children will imitate these simulated violent acts. The danger for the rest of our children is that they will build up a tolerance for violence; it will seem like a reasonable response to life's problems.

Just last week, a 15-year-old boy from upstate lost some of his vision after he was shot in the eye by a BB in a teenage war game. The boy was a "War Hawk" fighting against another youth group called the "Shock Troops of Hate."

One kid said all the guys can hardly wait till they "fight the Russians."

In three years, these kids will be voting and they talk about war as if it's akin to playing the Pittsburgh Steelers. And why not? Football — a territorial war game — has taken over from baseball as our national pastime.

Hey, I'm not coming on as the purist in this thing. The other week, I was watching boxer Boom Boom Mancini beat up on challenger Bobby Chacon. For a split second, I felt a little cheated when they stopped the fight in the third round. A guy already has died in the ring with Mancini. What the hell was I thinking about?

As sophisticated as we are, there's hardly a civilized country in the world that has the love affair with violence we Americans have.

The knee-jerk response is to ask government to ban what we find offensive. But we don't need a change of laws about violence; we need a change of heart.

We don't need to take control of what's on television; we need to take control of our children.

Who said they have to watch TV till their eyes fall out? Who said they have to grow up as listless consumers of violence without an idea in their head?

For their sake, we must turn them away from violence. History tells us a society that worships violence is living on borrowed time. Because a people that adores brutality is easily controlled by it.

Maybe the Record used poor judgment in printing an ad that appeals more to the madman than the sportsman. But the worst part is that so few of us seem to care.

We at least need to get to the point where a "Psycho Selloff" on guns upsets us at least as much as the televised picture of a naked body.

Chapter 5:

Parenthood

"There's a healing power in a baby's smile."
— Mike Levine, 1986

One in a Series of Firsts

I once cradled a helpless baby in my arms.

I held his bottle so he could eat. The only sound he could make was a cry for mommy and daddy. We lay him down on a tiny blanket and we knew he could not wander.

Now he is walking down the hill with his mom and dad and his little brother. He wears a blue backpack for his journey to the school bus.

I was warned about this day. Tough guys I know admitted they were knocked for a loop seeing their child go off to kindergarten. Things are never the same after this, they said.

Why, I would ask.

You'll see, I was told.

"I can hardly wait for the bus," said my boy, in a skip of a walk. "Can you hardly wait, too?"

Good question.

The day he first crawled, we made Kodak richer. His first word required instant wake-up calls to sleeping relatives.

There are no cameras, no phone calls today. It is only for the mother and father to share this great lonesome moment.

At the bus stop, he meets another boy sitting on the sidewalk curb. He sits beside him. They tell each other they're five years old and that seems to be enough of a bond for a curbside friendship.

They crane their necks in search of anything yellow and moving. "When is the bus coming?" asks my boy. His arms are spread, like he's ready to fly.

I used to look at him and see me. Sometimes, he would smile a certain way and I would see his mom or my father or my nephew.

Now I only see him. More and more, there are parts of himself only he owns, parts mommy and daddy cannot know. Or maybe I'm just coming to recognize it.

Just yesterday, he told his mother, "I'm not a stranger in this world, you know."

He and his new friend are occupied practicing new and strange "boy" sounds. The only thing they want to know from their parents is, "Is it a big bus or a small bus?"

It is a late bus. I look at my wife and recall the night we first met. I recall the wedding and the birth and that first cry of life we created.

Don't wish this time away, friends said when we complained about the baby keeping us up all night. You have control now. They fly away soon enough to meet the great unknown.

My boy and his new friend are practicing jumping off the curb. For the third time I hear myself say, "Hey, don't..."

"Daddy, when is the bus coming?"

Soon, soon. His younger brother strains to get out of his stroller. We tell him no, not now.

"Here comes the bus!" I say, spotting it way up the street. My son sees it and becomes quiet.

A big, yellow machine chugs to the corner and puts on its flashers. Traffic stops.

"Have a ball, son," I say giving him a hug.

He pulls away and disappears into the belly of the bus.

He gets to a window and waves. He wears a nervous smile of uncertainty and excitement, the look of a boy taking his first bike ride.

The bus goes away. His mother starts to cry. So does his little brother. I hide myself under a deep breath.

I once held a helpless baby in my arms. He cried when the lights went out and we would rock him. I saw a little of that scared look when the bus pulled away.

As the bus turned the corner, I wished I was still hugging him.

It's just that today there is more love in waving goodbye.

Precious Days

The young musician was down to eating onion sandwiches when a composer named Kurt Weill gave him a job conducting a Broadway show.

As the opening night reviews came in, Weill's wife, Lotte Lenya, told the musician the show was a hit. That meant the young musician would have a steady job. "Go home with your wife and make babies," she said.

A baby came along two years later. By then, Weill had died. The musician and his wife remembered the composer by giving their son the middle name of Kurt.

I liked having Kurt in my name. Whenever "Mack The Knife" came on — it was a big hit during my youth — I'd tell my friends I was named after the guy who wrote it.

But another popular Weill song seemed to me dark and distant. It started out like this: Oh, it's a long long time, from May to December; and the days grow short, when you reach September.

What was this? A nursery rhyme about the calendar?

When the autumn weather, turns the leaves to flame; one hasn't got time, for the waiting game.

What's the singer's worry? There's always another autumn.

The song puzzled me even more in 1965 when as a 13-year-old, I saw Lotte Lenya on stage at a Kurt Weill memorial tribute at Lincoln Center. Lenya, by then 67 years old, spread out her hands and sang "September Song":

And the days dwindle down to a precious few September, November... Watching Lenya, many in the audience wept. It was beyond me.

I saw Lenya next in September of 1980. My editor thought it would make a good, fall feature — an interview with Lotte Lenya talking about "September Song."

I drove down the Hudson Valley to Rockland and sat with Lenya on her back porch. She was 82. I was 28. She once sang me to sleep when I was a baby, but now we had little to say.

We looked out at the backyard meadow where Kurt Weill and Maxwell Anderson wrote "September Song." The song had been recorded by hundreds of singers. I asked her which one she liked the best. "Walter Huston," she said. He sang it shortly before his death in 1950, the same year Kurt Weill died.

"Walter didn't have a singing voice," she said. "But he understood the song." Especially the part where the song dismisses young love as "a plentiful waste of time of day."

I had an uneasy feeling on the way home. I had made more "plentiful wastes of time" than I could remember. Careless, casual mistakes I never looked back on. Hell, I was always young. I had time to burn. I wondered if something wasn't slipping by.

Lenya died that following autumn. I managed to escape my 20s. A few years later I married a wonderful woman. We had Benjamin in July 1985. Two years later, we were expecting a second child, confident and sure.

When we lost that baby, I never knew such sadness.

Last year, we nervously awaited the arrival of another child. It was no longer a sure thing. Samuel Walter came along in the first hours of a cool September morning.

The other week, the family was visiting relatives at Wolf Lake. It was a brilliant, crisp late summer's day. We were all saying there won't be many more like it.

My 4-year-old was trying to scoop tiny fish with a pail. The 1-year-old was tottering along the grass, his sea legs still unsteady, squeezing a carrot in his hand. My wife was rocking a newborn nephew to sleep. High on the treetops, a few leaves singed with red.

I saw it all. I held that moment like I never held one before.

Perhaps for the first time, I savored what life had given me. I savored it all the more knowing it would pass as swiftly and surely as the seasons.

For loss surrounds us like a forest of falling leaves.

Weill is dead. So is Lenya. My father, the young musician Lenya told to go home and make babies, is 71. His son will go his way and so will mine.

All the more reason then to number our days wisely, to seize the moment for joy.

And these few precious days I'll spend with you.

These precious days I'll spend with you.

I'm beginning to understand "September Song." It sings of the time when we are ready, at last, to live.

A Tortured Father Holds Out Hope for Lost Son

October 15, 1993

On this busy weekday, I beg your time for a small story. It's a midweek tale, in fact, a story of unfinished business. You might recognize something in it:

When the child was born, the father was working on Broadway. The message came from a stagehand and the cast shouted, "It's a boy." The birth announcement in the paper recorded the date as May 2, 1952.

The father and the son enjoyed each other's company when they could find it. They threw a ball to each other. They finished each other's punch lines. And exit lines.

The father's job sent him traveling. From city to city and sometimes country to country. Father and son would talk on the phone, trying to fill the missing blanks — the big base hit, the third-grade play, you should've seen it, dad.

Sorry I missed it, he told his son. He really was. But business was uncertain and he had to take every job.

One time, it was the fall of 1963 to be sure, the father took his son with him on business to Mexico. Faded photographs will record they were in paradise. They told a million jokes. They shared one day into the next until the days and the souls were one.

Before they left, the father said they must do this more often. Make time to spend together. He meant it, too.

Nothing changed. He got busy again. And so did the son.

Dear reader, you know all about the teenage years. You can imagine the son staked out his own turf. You can imagine the father wanted to know where his happy, adoring boy went.

Sparks flew. Sometimes they'd meet for summer walks and the father would give pedantic lectures on life. Most walks, they said nothing and missed each other.

They came together by the time the son was 21. It was the old tale about the son who says when he was 15 he thought his father a fool, but now at 20, it's amazing how smart his father got.

Maybe the father was smarter. He was divorced by then and he had given up his certainties. The two men enjoyed each other's company when they could find it.

Which wasn't often. They were busy hustling livelihoods. As both were allergic to money, this took up quite some time.

They got caught up in weekday things. Deadlines, deals, damsels. Very pressing matters, they said.

Weeks would go by without a word. They felt guilty when they talked on the phone. Instead of doing things together, they merely talked about making plans.

They swore they would go to the ball game together soon or grab a bite to eat or go to Israel, for crying out loud. Neither had ever been there. Soon, they agreed, just as soon as this busy period ends.

One busy night in 1979, the son got a call from the father's apartment. He got to the building in time to jump into the ambulance. The father and son spent the ride to the hospital together and even shared an old joke before the father slipped into a coma.

It was a stroke. The doctors told the son his father would die. The son shook with a little boy's sobs.

When the father stubbornly survived, with slurred speech and halting walk, they both agreed. No more putting things off. Life is short.

They'd spend a chunk of time together like they did in Mexico. As soon as everything got back to normal.

And when it did, they forgot their plans. They talked every week, then every month or so. It has gone on like this for near another 15 years.

The father is 75. It is now all he can do to walk across a room. He is still busy trying to make a living.

So is the son. And with the family and all, hey, dad, let's try sometime soon. He always meant it, too.

They said hi on the phone as the hour grew late. It seemed only death would bring the survivor to his senses. And fill him with unspeakable regret.

That's when an angel in the family gave the two men a gift. Thirty years to that week in Mexico when father and son made their vow to be together again, she would see that their promise was kept.

The angel made the arrangements in a hurry. Before time ran out. Because she understood time is always running out and we are too busy with our weekdays to know it.

Is this story familiar? Don't you have some unfinished business of life with someone special? A sentence, a kiss, a journey to complete?

Go ahead. Finish your business before it is too late. Don't depend on a heavenly hand to bring you together.

The father and son in this story got lucky. They united in time. This very weekday morning, they are touching the earth of Israel, promised land of their fathers, promised land of their sons.

May you and your loved ones stay well until your connection is complete. See you in two weeks.

From Fatherhood to Misunderstood

Once we were idealized in "Father Knows Best." Wise old dad was built from granite. He didn't say much but, gosh darn, when he did, he was as all-knowing as The Almighty.

Then came the backlash and the Father Knows Nothing movement. Dad was seen as a dictator who oppressed everyone around him. He was nailed as stern and rigid and cruel.

Pop culture's latest spin is "Dad — The Well-Meaning Oaf." This year's Father's Day commercials were all about taking dad to his favorite "toy" store as if he were a boy to be pacified. So if your befuddled Dagwood Bumstead gets cranky or overtired, humor him with a big screen TV so he can sit and drool like the nice family dog.

And what's on TV? Sitcom dads played as confused and easily manipulated half-wits.

More and more, children's books make dad sound like an afterthought or a boob. (The only mature adult in the Berenstain Bears is usually Mama Bear.)

Don't blame real-life mothers for this demeaning portrayal of fatherhood. Mothers know the value of a good father. But because women make most of the purchasing decisions in this country, the marketing geniuses' way of flattering mothers is to belittle fatherhood.

Hey, we'll survive. But just to set the record straight, most men I know consider fatherhood their most important job. Fathers aren't befuddled — they're trying to pull off the same crazy balancing act as everyone else.

Today's fathers often sacrifice career advancements to be with their children. This rips men apart because their instinct to provide is as deep-rooted as their breath. For most fathers, their sense of responsibility runs so hot, the stress sears the heart.

I see them worried about their jobs where they're forced to spend more and more time.

What happens if their paycheck goes up in company smoke? But if they work all hours, they're missing the chance to help prepare their kids for this crazy world.

What do you think goes through a man's head on his way to that second job or on the long ride home on Metro North? Leaving at 5 a.m., getting back after dinner, feeling like half a stranger in his own home.

And when fathers come home, most of them toil in the gritty details of child-rearing. The days when fathers left the kids to mom are over.

It's not all grim. Fathers have a deep, joyful instinct to teach. They never seem so happy as when they're hanging out and teaching kids in that easy, upbeat way of daddydom.

You see them out there on Little League fields, wired from a hard day's work, patiently showing a lost kid how to catch a baseball. You see them running into school auditoriums to catch the play. You see them hugging, horsing around, helping a kid in the secret language of daddy cool.

You see them on ponds with fishing rods surrounded by a gaggle of children. Here's how you reel it in. Go ahead, kid, you try now.

Sometimes being a father is a casting out. No, sweetie, you have to keep walking into that school. Be brave.

And be quick. All the time, fathers are looking at their watches. There's so many ways we burn to provide.

Fathers see the world. We see our jobs with our children. To protect and prepare, to set boundaries and to point out possibilities, to shelter and to set loose. To do everything well and at once, to always have our hand out in the wild currents that pull our children along too fast.

Yep, sometimes fathers can look goofy trying to balance everything. We may not always do a great job. But most men I know would die trying.

In Her Eyes, You'll Always Be the Best

May 14, 1995

My mother called from her sick bed last week. She had news. She was at the airport when who should she spot but Mario Cuomo.

She began to walk toward him. I don't know about this, my sister said. No, don't stop me, said my mother. She had something important to tell Mario Cuomo.

"Governor," she said, stopping him in his hurried tracks. "I am Mike Levine's mother."

This, my mother believed, would somehow impress a man who walks in the company of presidents and world leaders. And according to her, it did.

"He said you were a terrific writer, an incredible journalist and a good-looking boy," my mother told me. "He also said I looked young enough to be your sister."

Ah, politicians, I thought to myself. It's true my mother is a youthful beauty for her 73 years, but the former governor's compliments about me were certainly a gracious indulgence for a mother's benefit. I had but a few dealings with Cuomo and, despite my admiration for his bedrock decency, I was told I had irked him with some critical columns.

"He thinks you're brilliant," my mother assured me. I'm certain she was now breaking the Cuomo story to distant relatives and captive cab drivers.

So a few days ago, I had to call Cuomo for a column I was working on. I left a message with him and in return, he left a message on my voice mail.

"Is this the Mike Levine with the young mother?" thundered the voice that once moved a nation. "And am I to believe her when she says you're a terrific writer and a talented, handsome journalist?"

I shook with laughter. I called my mother. "Mom, Mario Cuomo didn't say those nice things about me to you. You said them to him."

"Oh no," she said. "Those things were said."

By whom, I asked.

"So how are you?" asked my hoarse mother. "Are you eating?"

Anyone who's ever been a child knows this story to be 100 percent true. There is something of a mother's love that is not in the realm of reality. When it comes to her children, she doesn't face facts. Every mother's child happens to be unbelievably smart, talented, sensitive and athletic. And she's not just saying that because it's her child. It happens to be true. A mother's love is so beautiful because deep down she has faith in her child.

Not that this is always easy to give or to take. Even Quaker moms can jump ugly with a Little League umpire who has the nerve to call her child out. And let's face it — in a mother's eyes, a child is 3 years old for the rest of his life, even when he's 60.

Like many mothers, mine can be a maddening worrywart. In the span of five minutes, she can worry needlessly about me and her grandchildren, our driving in the rain, our sitting too long in the sun, our apparent lack of food, my eating too much, their ears, one stray sneeze, their Little League batting averages and the threat of neo-Nazis.

But when real trouble comes, my mother is amazingly calm and understanding. She feels for me. There is never a doubt in her mind I am special, more so than any objective evidence would declare.

The girl that gets you is going to get a real bargain, my mom told me once. Mom, I said, nobody's any bargain. You're a bargain, she said.

I'm really not. Naturally, a boy has to break away from a mother's fussiness. It's healthy to learn the world's hard lessons and rough judgments.

When I finally connected with Mario Cuomo, he joked again about my mother's testimonial. He paused, and it did not dawn on me that he had just buried his mother. The next words Mario Cuomo spoke about my mom's performance were almost reverent. "I found it touching," he said.

So do I. It is a blessing to be cherished simply because you exist. To be touched by a mother's tenderness is to be touched by the love of the Creator of all life.

Which is to say, Happy Mother's Day, mom, and to every mother out there. In fact, I just heard from the president that you're the best, most beautiful mom ever.

The Kids Are Going to Be Okay...Really

September 7, 1994

Like most folks, I was an expert at raising kids before I had them. I actually remember telling a friend that my kids wouldn't ever whine. Pretty funny.

After learning I didn't know much, I depended on other so-called experts with academic titles. Surely, they'd tap into some universal truth. I found out these expert types can't agree on what time it is.

Now I know that when it comes to raising kids, there are no experts. We all give it our best shot and hope for the best. The best advice I've received is from other parents who've been there.

With school starting this week, I've collected a potluck basket of common sense tips from seasoned parents. This is an accumulation of wisdom about raising schoolkids from parents who now have grown children.

For those of us still going through it, I pass them along. Hey, the way the world and the schoolyard is today, we could use some timeless advice. Maybe a few of these tips will ring a bell with us.

1. They're going to be OK.
2. The sneakers don't matter.
3. Ask your kids what they did in school today and they'll say "nothing." Don't get alarmed.
4. Keep listening.
5. Give them a chance to fight their own battles.
6. Take everything your school district says with a grain of salt.

7. Meet the teacher early on and try to become partners.

8. Children don't need to come from Ozzie and Harriett families to succeed.

9. Every child needs someone at home saying and showing how important school is.

10. If you want to know how relaxed your kids are in school, check out their moods on Sunday nights.

11. Check their homework without fail; don't let them con you into doing it for them.

12. Ask your children to teach you what they're learning.

13. Connect with other parents in your child's class.

14. Really, they're going to be OK.

15. If you want your kids to get smarter, cut their TV time. It really works.

16. Let them see you read for pleasure.

17. Make sure they have giggle time.

18. Tap into their enthusiasm about anything in school. If they show an interest in animals, take them to the zoo or a nature trail.

19. Tell the teacher if you think there's a problem.

20. Trust your instincts.

21. If you want to know whether they're faking a stomach ache, look at their eyes instead of a thermometer. You know your kids; you can tell if they're sick, goofing off or scared of something in school.

22. Yes, they will learn the words you've been keeping them away from.

23. They'll survive it.

24. Let them kick back on weekends; it's a long school week.

25. Don't reward good grades with money or lavish gifts; instead, give them more privileges and tell them they earned it with their hard work.

26. If you want to know how your kid is doing, check out his or her friends. Their choice of friends will tell you all you need to know.

27. Be careful you don't succumb to peer pressure from other parents; that will send a message to kids about caving in to their friend's demands.
28. Don't let them kid you; children crave structure.
29. Reject any advice that doesn't sound right to you.
30. For the last time, they're going to be OK. A happy school year to all.

One Small Link to the Saner Side of Life

Everyone has those burnout days. Wednesday was one of mine.

A jangle of phone calls. Shouting, lonely, desperate messages. Letters to answer. Appointments to keep. Errands to run. Anger to swallow. Bills to pay. Columns to write. I felt scattered and burdened.

After dark, I walked out into the rain to go home. I couldn't shake the day. There was a buck thirty-five in my pocket and I felt lousy that there wasn't more. I wanted to buy my wife something pretty. Hell, I had just enough gas to get to the house.

I walked into the house empty-handed, weighing a ton.

Across the room in a walker was Benny, my 6-month-old son. He reached out his arms and flashed the world's biggest ear-to-ear, glad-to-be-alive smile.

All the poison of the day drained away. The knot in the stomach, the pain in the head, disappeared. My heart, which had been missing all day, began to beat.

***

Six months into my rookie season as a father, I'm just discovering what you parents out there already know. There's a healing power in a baby's smile. You also know something else this greenhorn is just learning? Being a parent changes your life forever.

It's certainly changed mine. Oh, I'm not talking about leading a more structured life or learning the fine points of diaper wipes. It's something else.

I just feel connected to the world differently.

For instance, when I read about that 4-year-old boy in Newburgh, tortured and battered to death, I reacted as anyone in their right mind would, with horror. But it also hit the parent in me. The moment after I read the article about the boy, I had to go hold my son.

And that 14-year-old boy murdered in Middletown. I imagined what it would be like to have my son disappear in stab wounds, autopsy reports, headlines, murder statistics...oh, my God.

It reminded what my mother always said whenever she heard of something terrible happening to a child. "Oh, those poor parents," she would say. Now I know what she means.

Any discouraging news about the world hits me harder now. The terrorist madness, the decline in values, the gimme-gimme attitude TV instills in children, scares and infuriates me.

My God, I think to myself, that's the world my Ben will be going into.

I realize I've got to work to make it better. That's part of my mission as a parent.

So, I find myself doing my job with a greater intensity. I leap at the chance to talk at local schools about writing and the joy of reading. I look to hook up with people who haven't given up on the future.

I've become a fan of anyone or anything that makes the world kinder or better. I'm cheered by people who do their job well. Carpenters, teachers, truck drivers, file clerks. Mothers. Mothers are incredible. My wife conducts herself as a loving mother with an elegance and grace more beautiful than anything I have ever seen in my life.

When I was 17 and knew it all, I got my philosophy off of posters: "I do my thing and you do yours and if by chance we meet..."

As a parent, I now find that nonsense. Sure, there's plenty of room for fun and individuality. But I think our true mission is to make the world better for our sons and daughters, and all the sons and daughters who will share the world with them.

We're here to connect; not separate.

My son is connected to his dead great-grandfathers who sailed to Ellis Island, who toiled in the rail yards of Orange County. My son is connected to his relatives who died in the concentration camps of Auschwitz. I look at Benny and realize their hearts have never stopped beating.

Yes, being a parent has changed my world. In some humbling and liberating way, life has begun to make sense.

Mother's Bond: Gift Hallmark Can't Top

May 9, 1999

Only by seeing the shadows did I come to see the light. The light revealed a secret. The secret is passed on.

For most of my adult life, my mother and I would touch base once a week. We inquired about each other's well-being. We were kind and polite, skimming the surface of our lives.

As with many adult children and their mothers, ours was a relationship to be maintained, not explored.

Three years ago this spring, my mother was diagnosed with advanced cancer. Pretense shattered. We moved forward.

I asked her about her life. Her childhood, her deepest wishes. I really listened and I came to know my mother.

I remind her of her hard-won accomplishments, marvel at her great warmth, salute her resilience. I am no longer driven by the teenage son's drive to escape mushy stuff with mom. We end every conversation with "I love you."

The secret is that there is a holy bond between a mother and the life she nurtured. It can be covered by pain or damage or starchy pleasantries but it still remains. This bond links us with our past and our children and allows us to feel a part of a great lifeline of light.

This mystery cannot be trusted to Hallmark or reduced to Freud. It must be explored with our own words and actions. Sometimes this takes courage.

I wouldn't wish illness on any family. I do root for every parent and adult child a chance to take a closer look at each other. You never know what treasures you might find.

I know people who are still angry that their mothers or fathers fell far short of perfection. They might not make the Mother's Day call today or if they do, they'll see it as an obligation to be weathered. They worry about old buttons pressed or the distance that has grown or they still fester over childhood disappointments.

Maybe it's time to move forward. Ask friends who no longer have their mother what they would give for one last conversation. To say the things they always meant.

To thank her for giving you life. To thank her for trying so hard. To thank her for believing in you.

To forgive her. To forgive yourself. To tell her what you see in her that you see in your children.

I don't know how the conversation begins. Maybe ask her for stories about her life. Listen without judgment. Look for the triumphs. See if resentments melt.

At the very least, the journey will lead to understanding. In time, you may come to love your mother the way she always loved you. Without condition.

I'm glad for the chance to know my mother this way. Sometimes the prospect of separation is so painful we distance ourselves again and pretend everything will always be just another day. Then we get back to the nitty-gritty.

I tell her that her gifts have been passed on. She counts her blessings. And though the shadows gather, we are forever heading for the light.

Chapter 6:

Life in the Hudson Valley

"The best thing I can say about this area is that I can't figure it out. The Catskills and the Hudson Valley are mystifying, aggravating, beautiful, ugly, maddening, rich, poor, cranky, hard-working, growing, dying, thoughtless, sentimental, rambunctious...add another 20 descriptions, and you still don't have it all."   — Mike Levine, 1988

You Can't Beat This Market's Selection

May 8, 1988

The calls started coming in the night I got back. A notice in the newspaper had said that I was on "special assignment." Sounded pretty jazzy.

Where had I been, the callers wanted to know? Lebanon? Somewhere in the Andes Mountains, cracking the Colombian dope connection? Getting to the bottom of the Tawana Brawley story?

"Uh, er, um," I mumbled in embarrassment. "I was at a seminar."

A seminar, they sneered? Snicker, snicker.

All right, already, lay off. For the past couple of weeks, I've been on "Get Smart" duty. The Record dispatched me to Virginia to a 10-day conference of editors from 32 major newspapers throughout the U.S., Asia and Central America. The management here was hoping all these bright people would rub off on me.

Fat chance.

They certainly had some smart folks there. Take the discussion about products and newspaper markets.

"Products" and "markets" are the current industry terms for newspapers and readers. The editors from the other products had their markets identified.

For instance, Fort Lauderdale and Fort Myers know they cater mostly to snowbirds and retirees. The Washington, D.C., paper understands it's writing to government workers. The Omaha paper serves a homogenous group of middle Americans.

And so, various members of the American Press Institute seminar asked me, what's this mid-Hudson market like?

Well, I said, it's interesting.

Interesting is not a marketing term, I was told. Was it upscale or downscale, I was asked?

Both.

Rural or urban or suburban?

All three.

Primarily senior citizens?

Well, we have plenty of older people, but we have more and more young ones, too.

It went on like this for 10 days. I kept trying to sum up the mid-Hudson "market." Well, let's see, we have Hasidim and Hutterians, streetwise New Yorkers, farmers with horse sense, Wall Street commuters and commune members, correction officers, stockbrokers, forest rangers.

We have every ethnic and religious group, Republicans and Democrats, Socialists and Falwell fundamentalists. We have mountains and valleys and two mighty river cultures, as different as they are mysterious.

The more I talked about Orange, Ulster and Sullivan counties, the harder it became to put a finger on our "market."

It began to dawn on me. We don't have a "market" we can target. We only have a lot of different people.

What a relief.

The best thing I can say about this area is that I can't figure it out. The Catskills and the Hudson Valley are mystifying, aggravating, beautiful, ugly, maddening, rich, poor, cranky, hard-working, growing, dying, thoughtless, sentimental, rambunctious...add another 20 descriptions, and you still don't have it all.

Certainly, Florida gets more sun, L.A. has more glitter, New England has more charm. We don't always get along, but we don't have to be the same to live together. Our strength is in our differences.

I got back from the seminar and opened my mail. The first letter was from a Philip Herbst in Highland Mills. "I still think you're a muddle-headed liberal," he wrote. "But your column on bilingual education shows that you apparently do have a brain. I'm beginning to like you, God help me."

The market in the mid-Hudson is people. Gee, but it's great to be back home.

Mid-Hudson Should Hop on the Secession Bandwagon

November 23, 1990

Just this month, Staten Island took the first steps to secede from New York City. This week, a group from several Adirondack towns said they were looking to secede from New York state and become part of nearby Vermont.

Let's not be last on line here. Ladies and gentlemen of the mid-Hudson/Catskills, opportunity knocks.

Now's our chance to secede from New York.

Lookit, we have state taxes coming out of our ears. They are the highest in America.

We're crushed under the weight of government regulations.

The state's credit rating is so bad, it couldn't get a Sears card.

We have a state Legislature that is the most expensive and wasteful in the 50 states. The mid-Hudson presence in that Legislature is zippo. If you're not living in New York City, Long Island or Buffalo, you get Bo Diddley from Albany.

And now we're going to get hit with state job cuts.

Who needs it?

Nothing in the Ten Commandments says we have to belong to New York. We can join Pennsylvania, which borders Orange and Sullivan counties. Pennsylvania seems like a nice, sane state with fairly low taxes.

Sounds good to me. So I call up Pennsylvania Governor Robert Casey in Harrisburg to plead our case for political asylum. Or at least I try to.

The operator gives me an 800 number for the governor. The only problem is that it can't be dialed from New York. There is no other number, she says.

You mean no one can call up the governor's office from out of state?

That's right, says the operator.

Terrific. I explain to her we're political prisoners in New York state. We seek asylum in Pennsylvania. She gives me the number for something called the Governor's Action Line. I call up.

I get a recording and get put on hold. For 4 minutes, 50 seconds. I finally get someone in the governor's press office. I explain our desperate situation. I remind her of their slogan, "You have a friend in Pennsylvania." I ask if we would be welcome to join their state.

She put me on hold. Someone named Taylor is supposed to get right back. I'm still waiting.

Cheez, their government is even dopier than New York's. At least in Albany, they have the courtesy to hang up on you.

Forget Pennsylvania. Who wants to root for the Phillies, anyway? And Jersey's out. We have some pride left.

We'll go it alone if that's how it must be. We've gotta be we, free as can be.

I hereby declare the birth of the new state Delason. It will be made up of the counties bordered by the Delaware and Hudson — our own Orange, Sullivan and Ulster. Any other county wants to get in, we'll charge 'em big bucks, like the NFL.

And so (drum roll, please), in the name of the great State of Delason, I hereby declare all our debts to New York null and void.

Worried about losing your New York state government job? No sweat. We'll contract out with Albany to run the existing New York programs here.

In time, we won't need those jobs, anyway.

With favorable tax rates, the State of Delason will attract blue chip businesses. We'll use taxpayers' money wisely, putting it back into sane things like housing, job training, health care. No bloated state legislature, no wasted dollars, no wasted forests from the paperwork of a useless bureaucracy.

The State of Delason is ready to roll.

We got a major airport in Stewart. We got nature. Anyone wants to mess with us, we got West Point to back us up.

As for money, we got Tuxedo Park. And anyone wants to starve us out, we got onions.

As a separate state, Delason can get federal funding. We'll have our own U.S. senators.

Start sending in your petitions, your nominations for a state bird. Delason needs a motto, a state flower, state bug, someone to design a flag.

We will not be deterred in our fight to unshackle our chains. If at first we don't secede, we'll try, try again.

I know not what course others may take but as for me, give me Liberty or give me Chester.

Answers to Tourists' Most Pressing Questions

June 26, 1988

The mid-Hudson-Catskill tourist season is in full swing. Welcome one and all.

Folks from around the nation come here to enjoy our mountains, outdoor recreation and historical attractions. Of course, that doesn't explain why the most common question travelers ask is, "Where's Playtogs?"

Like most of you full-time residents, I can't wait to show off my hometown region. As a helpful guide to visitors, I've compiled a list of the most frequently-asked questions about our area. I've even included some handy answers.

Are stores in the mid-Hudson open on Sunday?

It is illegal for a mid-Hudson store to ever close. Like Philadelphia is the City of Brotherly Love, the mid-Hudson is the Region of Perpetual Shopping.

At 2 a.m., you can buy underwear, pot roasts, electric razors and sneakers.

As former children of the '60s, we went to Woodstock to search for the site of the famous festival. Where is it?

Common mistake, travelers. The Woodstock festival was not held in the Ulster County town of Woodstock, but in the Sullivan County town of Bethel, about 75 miles away. Some people there are still pretty sore about 400,000 people messing up their lawns. Do not ask for directions. They'll tell you to go to Woodstock.

Things seem a bit of a hodge-podge in the region. Are there any planning and zoning requirements?

Who's your lawyer?

What is the quality of life here?

Each community is a perfectly balanced gem of modern living. Take the Middletown-Wallkill area where there's a shopping strip on each end of town.

The two strips are a pair of matched bookends. Each has a McDonald's, a Burger King, a Wendy's, a Pizza Hut, a Dunkin' Donuts, a Rite-Aid, a Shop-Rite and a Hess station.

This sense of symmetry, of aesthetic balance, makes this place some kind of wonderful.

Our family came up here to get away from congested Long Island. All we've seen so far are condos and discount stores. Where does the country start?

About 10 miles north of Livingston Manor.

Where's the famous Black Dirt region of the mid-Hudson? What is it?

It's located in the onion-growing region of Pine Island. The area gets its name because the soil is black.

Isn't most soil black?

Mmmmmm.

We see all those stores off the highway exit marked "Middletown." This must be a busy city.

Actually, all those stores and condos you see from the highway are located in the town of Wallkill. The City of Middletown is now a pleasant residential suburb of the Route 211 shopping area.

Middletown is now celebrating its centennial as a former vital hub with the slogan "100 years is enough." Visitors are welcome. The city is open from 9 a.m. to 5 p.m. Monday to Friday.

What's that low rumbling noise we're always hearing?

That's the sound of people complaining. Next to shopping, it's our favorite pastime.

Why are so many people here in a bad mood?

Oh, shut up.

Our family's been traveling on Route 84 in eastern Orange County. Is there something wrong with our car or is it the road?

If you've been traveling on Route 84, there's something wrong with your car now. That particular road was part of an unsuccessful state plan to construct highways out of used razor blades.

Traffic on major roads gets backed up Sunday nights. Are there alternate routes to the Quickway and the Thruway?

Yeah, like we're really going to tell you.

Thanks for visiting. Come back soon, y'all.

Hail, Fallonia, You're Full of Baloneya

There might have been fireworks yesterday for you and me. But at Scott Moone's Town Pantry in High Falls, Independence Day was no big deal.

"Just another working day," said the co-owner of this Ulster County general store.

Don't think Moone doesn't love America. It's just that High Falls, a hamlet of several hundred people, is no longer in the United States. And, by the way, it is no longer called High Falls.

All hail, Fallonia!

Fallonia is the new nation in the heart of Ulster County. Moone and other revolutionaries of this "former" hamlet started this new country April 1. It's all in their Declaration of Independence (copies have been smuggled out of Fallonia and made public for the first time here).

"We hereby declare that the area known as High Falls, N.Y., henceforth shall be known as Fallonia, a sovereign nation, independent and free of the United States."

Why? Well it's all spelled out in their five-point declaration. There's a bunch of words about unfair taxes but by the fifth point, they get to the root of their reason. "Because we want to."

Great. Revolution for the hell of it.

"Originally, we just wanted to secede from New York, but we figured why not go the whole route?" said Moone.

High Falls depends on tourism; townspeople told the state it could stick its plans in it ear.

"We'll put a want ad in the paper for dioxin. We'll pour it all over town," Moone warned at the time. "Then we'll get the government to buy us out."

High Falls won the argument. The state backed down.

And then there's High Falls University. A while back, High Falls held a giant graduation exercise and party for the college graduating class. There was music and dancing and food. There were big signs saying, "Congratulations to High Falls University graduates."

Not one person seemed to mind that there is no High Falls University.

Next came the signs that appeared all over the hamlet for the High Falls subway system.

And now High Fallonians go on to bigger and better things — a country that doesn't exist.

"We'll be setting up a mint soon," said Moone. "Our currency is the fallon. Taxes, of course, will be voluntary."

Moone was asked if Fallonia was looking forward to fielding an Olympic team.

"No," he said. "We'd like a USFL franchise. No league is going anywhere without a solid team in Fallonia."

Sound like fun? Well, said Moone, a lot of people are stopping in the store requesting dual citizenship. "As soon as we print our stamps, we'll mail 'em out," he said. By the way, the Fallonia revolutionary council has decided that it won't be people's heads that are featured on stamps. "Another part of the body," is all he'll say.

Is all this silly? Nonsensical?

You bet, High Falls is one of the few remaining communities that still cherishes a great American trait — a sense of humor.

They remind us to raise the flag of laughter once in a while. "Maybe it's the air here or something," said Linda Murphy, who runs the Eggs Nest, a Fallonia gathering place. "But I guess we figure you only pass this way but once. You might as well have some fun."

In some carefree corner of our hearts, we are all Fallonians.

A Sullivan Twist of 'Irish' Camaraderie

March 16, 1983

Tony Cellini, an Italian delegate of the Sullivan County Sons of St. Patrick, is trying raise Richard Nixon the telephone.

"That's N-I-X-O-N, Richard Milhous, former president of the U.S., in Saddle River," Cellini told the information operator from his barroom pay phone.

Sullivan's 80-strong St. Paddy's "Sons" — at least five of them are actually Irish — are trying to do a good deed. Why not give a break to a guy down on his luck? Invite him to speak at the Sons' big annual breakfast.

But all Cellini gets is some sniffy Nixon aide in charging of taking calls from barroom pay phones. He is told the former cover-up king charges $50,000 per speaking engagement.

"That's what we get for doing a guy a favor," said Cellini.

So they decided to celebrate St. Patrick's Day minus the serpent.

Not that they need any headliners here. These Irish Sons — the Bernsteins, the Seletskys, the Cellinis and the Labudas — are their own top bananas.

They're the county's movers and shakers and they meet every St. Patrick's at Roark's Tavern to bury the hatchets they've thrown at each other the rest of the year.

Walk around the barroom and meet some of the rollers who make the Catskills shake.

Here comes Harry Seletsky, trumpets blaring. The Republican county chairman has only two tones of voice — scream and whisper. He leads with the louder.

"For crying out loud, why don't you write something nice about me for once!" shouts Seletsky, poking a finger into his victim's chest. Then in the next moment he is cooing softly about some juicy gossip.

The Don Rickles routine does not endear Harry to everyone. But his ability to get the votes out would be the envy of the late Mayor Daley.

The elfish dignitary by the phone booth is Monticello's "marryin' mayor," Lou Harmin. Hizzoner's idea of a good time is to send couples off into the land of happily ever after — 48 in one term at last count.

"My last marriage was a first for me," says Harmin triumphantly. "It was the couple's second marriage to each other in two years."

Over by the scrambled eggs, long-faced village manager Lou Bernstein sighs heavily. Bernstein doesn't just root for the Yankees. He worries for them. "They look good on paper but..." says Bernstein somberly, wearing the burden of Steinbrenner's millionaires on his shoulders. Bernstein should thank God he's not a Mets fan.

There's Dave Kaufman, the Thompson town supervisor, fidgeting uncomfortably over in a corner. Kaufman — a study in sobriety — looks out of place in any bar, let alone one owned by town Councilman Cellini.

The two are mad at each other only on days ending in y.

"Hiya Dave," the breezy Cellini says, extending his hand.

"Hello, Tony," says Kaufman stiffly.

They grasp hands. For a split second, they both smile.

There is sadness here. The two used to be friends. There was a political falling out and then a personal one. They are decent men who can't let go of their hurt.

And so these 80 men — a gathering of different drummers — continue into the Irish morning over bagels and sausage. They roast each other and laugh at themselves.

Later, they drive over to the real St. Patrick's parade to Yulan. There is talk about starting a Daughters of St. Patrick's next year and hey, why don't we do this more often, gentlemen.

But this morning, as always, some of these same men will stand in cranky circles. They'll grumble that hard times will cause Sullivan County to drop dead in its tracks at any moment.

It doesn't have to.

The strength of this county is its people. If they lived every day in the Sons of St. Patrick spirit of camaraderie, there would be no reason to worry.

When the Doctor Was Part of the Cure

September 23, 1984

Kids are wailing, bouncing, rolling home from the elementary school. Without a glance, they pass the house on 59 Linden Ave. It is a modest wood home on an old working-class street in Middletown.

This is the house where Hans Kulka lived and worked. This is the house once filled with children and working men, careworn mothers and old maids. Now, in the front yard, schoolkids horseplay under a naked wooden post where a shingle has been removed.

Hans Kulka was a family doctor. He made house calls. He charged the same for them as he did for office visits. At the close of his practice in 1983, his fee was $11.

He came to Middletown 34 years ago from Europe by way of New York. A neighbor remembers Hans Kulka saying he was a rebel as a youngster. But dozens of people I talked to this week remembered only a gentle, private man. They say the rebel in him must have remained in his stubborn refusal to turn away a patient.

If you had three kids and they all needed shots, he'd line 'em up in the office and charge you for one visit. Poor farm workers would pay him in onions, laborers in firewood, and the destitute with thanks.

For the benefit of the working person, he stayed open at night. No appointment necessary. Sometimes the crowd spilled onto the front steps.

"No one complained," says Eleanore Scott, 49, whose entire family were all patients of his. "Because when you finally went in to see him, he made you feel like you were the only one he had cared for all day."

Because Hans Kulka, a big man with a heavy German accent, owned the driest of humor. With a gentle straight-faced barb, he would remind his patients they were going to live. "I think the jokes were part of the healing," says Mrs. Scott.

Men and women, with no place else to bring their thoughts, told Hans Kulka their secret sorrows.

"People would come in and cry on his shoulder," says his wife, Gabrielle. "And they'd leave laughing. He told them a joke and he told them the truth. They trusted him."

So he would be the man called on to treat a fevered child in a Christmas Eve blizzard. He would be the man the parents of a teenager on drugs turned to for counsel. He would be the man who would set off in his old black Volkswagen bug to heal an elderly woman.

Mrs. Kulka watched her husband grow tired. Still, there were precious times in their modest weekend retreat in Sullivan County. They were a close family with a handful of good friends. But Hans Kulka was not a joiner of large groups. He preferred to walk with his camera and take pictures of sunsets.

It was at the weekend retreat where he became ill last year and was forced to retire. He never got used to it.

"I just don't understand why I'm not going to the office," Hans Kulka told his wife, shortly before he died last week at the age of 70.

***

Eleanore Scott has found a new doctor. She went for her first visit. He had her take this test and that test as a matter of routine for first time visits. The bill was $240.

There weren't even any jokes.

"Dr. Kulka was what a town should really be about," she says. "Where people aren't names out of a phone book. He made you feel like you belonged here. He was your doctor and your children's doctor. And you knew he cared if we lived or died."

They tell us we have more sophisticated medical treatment in town these days. But we don't know if more people are really getting better health care. And we don't know if we have a better town.

Because a town needs more than fancy medical equipment. It needs men like Hans Kulka, who we know will face a Christmas Eve blizzard to care for a sick child.

That's what makes home feel like home. And that's why so many of us, learning of Hans Kulka's death last week, felt terribly lost.

Area's Heritage Being Put Out to Pasture

February 8, 1989

Your town must have a place like the Distelburger farm. Some living watercolor of the past, a kerosene street lamp in a fluorescent world, waiting for the bulldozer and the history book.

From Middletown, folks motor past the Distelburger farm on their way to the mall. They see the slow-moving cows and the red barn right on East Main Street. They wonder how much longer.

Not much.

This week, news came that Distelburger's 44 acres are for sale. The owners are asking $6.6 million for their prime land near the intersection of the Route 17 and Interstate 84.

Not far away, tucked in a back road of Ridgebury, a mile and a half from the general store, it's close to milking time at the Gibbs farm.

The barn's on the left, rebuilt after a 1984 fire. The farmhouse, built in the 1750s by a man named Durland, sits across the road. Gary Gibbs, 10 years old, stands in its kitchen, about to start his afternoon chores.

"Well, let me think," he says, politely answering a visitor's question. "My father, my grandfather, and my great-grandfather."

This makes Gary the fourth generation of Gibbs farmers in Ridgebury and he wants to do it all of his days.

"I like cows," he says cheerfully, as if wondering who wouldn't. "And I don't like sitting around."

Gary gets ready to bound over to the barn to feed the calves. His father, Al, walks over with him and says, "It's a good life."

A car zooms by. He looks both ways when he crosses the road. "Never used to," says Al. "Never had to."

Gary shows off the calves. The barn fills with moos. He and his sisters have total responsibility for the 25 calves, their feeding, their care. He even helped deliver one a few months back.

He looks about as peaceful and busy as a 10-year-old boy could ever be. "My friends come here and they're kinda bored," he says. "They like games and computers."

His father wonders if the family would still be here if the barn had burned a year later in 1985, when the land market boomed. Maybe they wouldn't have rebuilt it. He could have sold out to the condo developers.

"The thing is our roots are in the area," he says. His folks live on a farm a mile away. His wife's family still farms in the Goshen area.

But this is no longer a world hospitable to farmers.

The agriculture program at Minisink High School, the one Al completed as a boy, was canceled this year.

Last summer, the boy showed his prized calf at the Orange County Fair. "The fair is a carnival now," says Al. He says the older kids must sleep near the animals to keep the drunks away.

Yet, every time the real estate people come by, Al keeps saying no.

"Farming's been good to this family," he says. "People say it's hard work. Yes, but you get to watch your kids grow up."

The afternoon is almost gone; the cows are ready to be fed. Al doesn't seem rushed. "If Gary wants to farm, I'd encourage him to go upstate," he says. "Or somewhere where they're more prone to farming."

We are now prone to shopping here, where glum-faced boys explore stores instead of barns. We are prone to moving in and out of condos that families will never pass on.

Only a generation ago, dairy farming families lived where the mall and the slip-knot of highway light the night. Now, the surrounding land is the province of developers and chain-store marketing men. What's indigenous to our area can find breathing room only on the back roads.

The main roads glitter. In the shadow of Distelburger, not a stone's throw away, they are putting the finishing touches on a major new mall.

The mall will be called Dunning Farms.

Tourist Quiz Was Real Trip

May 19, 1991

When times are hard, tourism brings easy money.

Tourists come looking to empty their pockets. They buy stuff they wouldn't buy at home. They pump money into a community faster than any other source.

That's why regions go crazy trying to promote tourism. Motel clerks and gas station attendants are trained to sell their area. Broken-down blocks are renamed "historic districts."

The Hudson Valley and Catskills should be a tourist mecca. We're the closest, most beautiful and affordable haven for weary city folk.

We have West Point, rafting and canoeing on the Delaware, wineries, Greenwood Lake, Sugar Loaf crafts village, boating on the Hudson, Museum Village, golf, harness racing, world-class hiking and fishing, lakes, George Washington's Revolutionary War Headquarters, ice caves, awesome landscapes. We have a philharmonic, first-run repertory theater, art galleries.

All a tourist has to do is ask. Right? Let's see.

Last week, I posed as a tourist looking to explore the sites of Orange, Ulster and Sullivan counties.

I called a dozen motels in the area and stopped by several gas stations. I told each one my family might be coming to the area for a weekend. What are the attractions?

Here are the top three tourist suggestions offered by Orange County motel clerks and gas station attendants:

1) Shopping centers.

2) West Point.

3) Bowling.

Nobody mentioned canoeing or rafting on the Delaware, Sugar Loaf, Greenwood Lake, golfing, Hill Hold Museum, art exhibits, horse farms, Museum Village, the Brotherhood Winery (the oldest in America), or the Hall of Fame of the Trotter.

I figured to have better luck in Sullivan County. After all, tourism is the lifeblood of these Catskill communities.

I called a motel across the street from Monticello Raceway. I said I was thinking of coming up for the weekend. What was there to do in Sullivan County? The clerk suggested a small amusement park near Fallsburg. He did not even mention the raceway across the street.

I called a motel in Liberty. I asked what there was to do. "Mountains," said the clerk.

That's the way to talk it up. No one in the Sullivan County motels I called mentioned Delaware River canoeing and rafting. No one mentioned historic battlefields, the covered bridges, the jazz festival in Tusten, the state parks, the golfing, the major hotel entertainment.

No one suggested calling the Sullivan County Office of Public Information, which is probably a good thing.

This week, a Record reporter called the county's public information office. He asked about visiting Minisink battlefield (a Revolutionary War landmark) and the Roebling covered bridge, a national landmark. When are these attractions open and how much do they cost, he inquired?

I don't know, was the official answer from the Sullivan County Office of Public Information.

On to Ulster County. Here's the suggestion of a Kingston motel when I asked what there was to do in the area: "I don't know — sightseeing."

That was the Cook's Tour compared to this response from a New Paltz motel. Anything to do in the area? "Yeah," said the clerk. "I guess." And then silence.

No one suggested Woodstock or Mohonk. Not one motel clerk suggested a call to the county's tourism office.

In a hard-pressed economy, this region is blowing money big time. We have a wealth of riches. We are within two hours' driving distance for 20 million people looking for a good time.

And yet the day before yesterday, a motorist walks up to a gas station attendant on Dolson Avenue in the heart of Orange County:

I'm up here for the day. Are there any interesting places to visit?

"How far you willing to drive?" asks the attendant.

Anywhere that's worth going to, says the motorist.

"Well, there's a mall."

Anything else?

"There's a movie theater on Route 211."

Any parks or anything?

"Yeah, some small ones. I guess there's not much to do here. I'm sorry."

We sure are. Found money is lost to our economy. What's worse is what our ignorance says to the world about our community pride.

Condoman Grips Bucolic Burg by Wallet

August 2, 1989

Shocking but true!

Every day, hundreds of development stories appear in mid-Hudson newspapers. And guess what?

Every development story says the same thing!

Yes, that's right. The developer promises the world and the opponent says it will mean the end of the world. Only the details change.

By now, we can all write the story ourselves. It's just a matter of filling in the missing blanks.

That's why you're invited to play "King Condo vs. the Not-In-My-Neighborhood gang — The One Size Fits All Development Story."

Take a glance at the story below. Just ask a friend to provide the part of speech indicated, like in those old Mad Libs games.

Complete the missing blanks and, presto, you've done it. You'll never have to read another development story again.

Developer unveils plans; residents protest

In front of (three-digit-number) screaming (name of mid-Hudson community) residents, developers announced plans yesterday to build the world's biggest (type of structure).

Seymour Con Jobbo, lawyer for (name of quick-drying glue) Developers, was pelted with (plural name of food) and (plural name of inanimate object) as he said the project will be a boon to the community.

"Residents should get down on their (plural anatomy part) and thank us," said Con Jobbo.

He said among other things the project will:

- Generate (number) billion dollars in local taxes every (number between one and 10) seconds.

- Create 5,000 (adjective) jobs while preserving the (adjective) character of the town.

- Be the most hopeful development in the world since (historical event).

Con Jobbo also said that while this project will bring in (six-digit number) additional (type of vehicles) to the town every day, it will have absolutely no impact on traffic.

Opponents, who are members of Citizens For A (adjective) Community, said their opposition is not a case of the "Not-In-My-Neighborhood" syndrome.

"It has nothing to do with wanting to keep our community all (name of ethnic group), (name of racial group) and (name of religious group), said one protester. "We simply want to preserve the rural character of our (adjective) hamlet."

"That's right, we're not anti-growth," said a cigar-smoking opponent. "We've always been concerned how development will impact the area's (name of insect) and the (name of poisonous snake) that we so dearly love."

Town (name of local political office), up for re-election this year, told protesting residents he was in their corner. "This (adjective) plan will (verb) our community. I am (any number above hundred) percent opposed. I will lay down in front of the (name of construction equipment) if they try to build."

An hour later, the same elected official emerged from a private meeting with Con Jobbo full of smiles and (sum of money) in cash.

"As (name of president who resigned in disgrace) said, I am not a (noun)," he said (adverb), before speeding away in his 1989 (name of foreign sports car). "I simply believe it is to time to (verb) our planning strategies, with controlled growth projects like these, so that we can prepare a better world for the (name of insect) and the (name of poisonous snake)."

Con Jobbo said the developers, with headquarters in the (name of former Yankee manager) Rest Stop on the New Jersey Turnpike, are not fly-by-night operators. "Come down and visit us at our post office box," said Con Jobbo.

The proposed project will need move into the next phase — an environmental impact statement on the (name of poisonous snake), a presentation before the town's (verb ending in ing) Committee on Studying Unreadable Studies and an extra $ (number in the hundred thousands) in Con Jobbo's legal fees.

Woodstock Era: Same Stuff, Different Decade

August 19, 1987

God save us from the media on slow news weeks. In between Elvis Presley anniversary death orgies, the press and TV have battered us with gibberish about harmonic convergences. We've also gotten sentimental stories about the 18th anniversary of Woodstock — peace, love and rock 'n' roll, the run-of-the-mill New Age bedtime stories.

The New Agers, who goof on the Presley crowd, talk about harmonic convergences with a straight face. They utter the word Woodstock as if something really sacred took place on that farm in Bethel.

Sue me, but as one of the 400,000 there that weekend, I remember Woodstock was about as holy as a Twinkie.

Like a lot of kids who drove upstate from the city neighborhoods, my friends and I went to the festival 'cause our favorite bands were supposed to be there.

I was 17 and I had saved a few bucks from my summer factory job. A hundred dollars got me a failing 1960 Valiant. We packed cream soda, some Twinkies, a few cans of tuna (forgetting a can opener) and puttered up the Thruway. We talked sports and girls.

The Woodstock nation. Peace and love. The dawning of a new age.

Yeah, right. We were about as revolutionary as Whitey Ford.

I almost fell asleep in the traffic jam along Route 17B.

When we finally got there, the music was great, although 400,000 people deep, it was like watching people from an airplane. The rains came. Everyone got butt-deep in mud.

It was a fun picnic but not everyone was going around saying it was the time of their lives.

How lasting an impression did Woodstock make? We left early and, on the way home, turned on the Jets-Giants exhibition game on the radio and talked Namath.

Woodstock? Oh yeah, that was OK. To the neighborhood guys, it meant nothing more to us than a rock concert, an amusing adventure.

That is until we got home and found out how the media had got hold of it. We saw pictures of naked hippies, kids flashing peace signs, acid-soaked druggies babbling that we were a new nation of peace-loving souls that would save the world. Hendrix playing the Star-Spangled Banner.

Woodstock became marketable as media myth. The movie. The record. The song. We ate it up. Gee, we were part of something important.

We began to kid ourselves about Woodstock. Yeah, that's right, it was magic. Peace, love. The Woodstock generation. We believed we were special.

Over the past 18 years, many of us in the "Woodstock generation" have made the journey upstate again.

We come as young parents, scraping up mortgage money, shopping for house-brand tuna with an eye on our kids' dentist bills. We slave for the kind of homes and the kind of lives some in the Woodstock generation had once made fun of.

This weekend the media asked its annual question — whatever happened to the Woodstock generation? The answer is nothing. We never really wanted anything much different from our parents.

We are shaped, not by rock concerts or some harmonic pie-in-the-sky, but by the forces that shaped our parents' lives — marriage, kids, aging, security. We possess no special magic to make life suddenly different.

It doesn't make us bad people. The music is still important to us, maybe even more so, because it serves as a real release from life's pressures.

A core of committed souls has stayed involved in issues. They do this by schlepping out after dinner to a meeting. It is hard work and no one's making a movie of it.

Our only chance to make the world better is through the same wearying, frustrating tool possessed by every generation: doing our best over the course of a lifetime.

The rock concert was nice, a weekend picnic. It had no lesson to teach us about life.

This time up the Thruway, the Woodstock generation is living the real adventure.

Disaster Realizes Every Mother's Nightmare

November 17, 1989

The mother's car is stuck in the long line of traffic and flashing lights and sirened police cars. Donna Ferguson of Rock Tavern cannot wait any longer.

She gets out, bundles 3-year-old Kelly in her arms, puts 5-year-old Tiffany alongside of her and begins to walk up the long hill. The school is almost a mile away, over the crest and out of sight.

"Chris," she says softly, saying her son's name.

Her mouth turns down and quivers as if crying, but no sound comes out. Her eyes are wildly vacant, beyond tears, turned inward to a terrible vision.

There is no look like it in God's creation. This is a mother's face when she does not know if her child is dead or alive.

Her legs march forward, little Kelly heavy on her chest. Tiffany chugs alongside. The sudden chill in the air slaps their faces red.

An ambulance races up the hill ahead of her.

The lips quiver again. "Jesus," says the mother.

She catches the kids looking at her and she tries to straighten out her face. It is no use.

Her mind races to find a memory of Chris that morning. What did she say to him before he went off to school with his little GoBot lunchbox? What was the hug like? She cannot remember.

Chris was always up for school. Such a little man, she thought. Her oldest.

Nine years old next week.

The mother recognizes a man walking down the hill.

"Lou, what's happening?"

The man looks like he is trying to couch his words. "Something about a tornado," he says. "The cafeteria caved in. They're taking kids to St. Luke's."

"Jesus Christ," moans the mother.

Her legs keep working up the hill.

Several mothers walk down the hill with their kids in tow. They walk down one side of the road.

The mothers on the way up walk on the other side. They do not ask any more questions. You see it on their faces.

Walking up that hill, every mother's child is dead.

Now the mother sees the East Coldenham Elementary School. The all-glass front of the building has been blown out. Shattered and splattered into the cafeteria as children ate lunch. A tornado someone describes as looking like a black band had ripped it apart.

"Jesus," says the mother. "Jesus Christ." Her head turns this way and that, everywhere at once, where is Chris? Where is her son? Where?

Through the mill of bodies and flashing lights, she sees Chris. He is standing on the side of the road, lunchbox at his side. She lets little Kelly down. Mouth open, arms out, she moves toward her son.

She gathers him to her bosom and she holds him there and, at long last, tears roll down her face and cries leap from her mouth.

Chris stands there numb. He answers questions.

He was taking a science quiz in Room 115, just before his time for lunch. He looked out the window and saw the trees bend and he heard the wind blow.

Then he was out in the hall.

Everyone was crying, he says, the kids and the teachers. He saw a friend of his, lying in the hall, blood flowing out of her.

The mother says she will take Chris home and hug him all day.

Her son walks down the hill toward the car, head bowed.

Down the hill in Coldenham, a pregnant mother walks into Tom's Deli with her sobbing 7-year-old daughter. A candy bar, a candy bar might make her feel better.

Calm down, dear, says Lisa Watkins softly from behind the counter.

"Kimmy's dead," weeps the little girl. "Kimmy's dead."

Oh, maybe she's really OK, says Ms. Watkins, maybe she's going to be fine.

"No," cries the girl. "Her back was ripped open. I saw her. She's dead."

Thankfully, she was not; she and 18 others were injured. Seven of her schoolmates had died.

In one terrible moment, all the children of East Coldenham Elementary School had known something that would forever change them. A mother could not chase it away.

The pregnant mother buys her 7-year-old girl a KitKat bar. The daughter keeps crying.

Candy bars and hugs, that was all the power a mother had.

Candy bars and hugs against the black band of death.

Chapter 7:

Grace, Gratitude and Connections Greater Than Ourselves

"The wonder is not that we die, but that we ever were."
— Mike Levine, 1999

Searching for Visions in Our Souls, Pocketbooks

September 30, 1999

An 81-year-old woman called on deadline to mourn a stolen pocketbook. She had cried for days, spent another week replacing her documents. She was still missing a precious piece of paper.

Would we put an item on the front page in the hope someone might return it?

I work for a newspaper. We deal in high crimes and twists of power. I was set to launch into our standard response, that while a stolen purse may be a deep personal loss, it was too minor a crime to be a news story.

She told me her name and asked me not to use it. One more reason, I decided, this would never make the paper. But a catch in her voice stopped me from telling her.

I stalled for time. Thinking there might be some special detail elevating this to news, I asked her to tell me more.

On the morning of Tropical Storm Floyd, said the woman, she went to the Price Chopper in Vails Gate to stock up.

Afterwards, she rolled her bags to the rainswept parking lot, her navy blue pocketbook in the small compartment of the cart. On unsteady legs, she pushed the groceries into the back seat.

When she turned around, her pocketbook was gone. She reported it to the police at once. Stolen was $75 in cash. Stolen was her driver's license. Stolen were her credit cards, her Social Security information.

That's not what made her weep. Someone had stolen her visions; a piece of paper deep in her pocketbook. She had compiled them over a lifetime, listed carefully by time and date.

There was the vision she had while she cared for her sister with cancer. She dreamed God spoke to her. "No knowledge will heal a broken heart. But suffering will." The vision gave her comfort as she had to watch her sister die.

Some visions brought back happiness. She was 8 years old receiving First Holy Communion and she felt she was flying to heaven. Another vision recalls her grandchildren, another her dead husband.

Each vision was recorded on the piece of paper, sparking memories each time she reached for them in her purse.

She does not grieve her lost money or charge cards or official documents. She grieves not being able to look at the words that tell her story. They are too personal, too precious to lose, too much a part of the book of her life.

What makes her think the thief would return the piece of paper? Because, she said, "the Commandments are written in our hearts."

Then surely these visions are etched in your soul, I said. Sometimes, she said, you need to be able to look at them.

Yes. We're dulled daily by facts and figures, reams of data rolling off the press, the Internet, pelting us at every turn like a storm. We count money, make a god of it, spend a lifetime in its pursuit.

What makes us alive, what binds one of us to the other, one generation to the next, are our singular small stories, our midnight dreams. These visions are windows allowing us to see eternal truths in our fleeting lives.

These truths are too big for the front page of a newspaper. These visions are not news, here today and gone tomorrow. If we're wise, they will linger for all of us on scraps of paper, tucked away in the bottom of dresser drawers, in dusty attics, deep in our pockets and purses.

As the Newburgh woman continues to search for her sacred visions, maybe we should spend time looking for ours.

The Lights of Christmas Present

December 19, 1999

Three years ago, I was teaching a writing course at Orange County Community College. One student introduced herself only as Peggy. She radiated kindness.

Isn't that Peg nice? I said to a fellow student during our first break.

You mean the nun, said the student. The nun? Yes, said the student, that's Sister Peggy Murphy.

Sister Peg bathed our class in light. Not that she went around with a halo and pat answers. She probed the darkest questions with intellectual gusto and got the joke every time.

She would beam at the sheer beauty of someone's well-written sentence. She discovered the worth in everyone's work and wrote stunning poetry herself.

Truth is, she became my teacher far more than I was hers. When the course ended, we went our separate ways.

One dark afternoon last fall, I was at work and feeling low. It was the first anniversary of my father's death. Out of the blue, I got a phone call from Sister Peggy.

She said she had been thinking of me and my father. She wanted to let me know how proud he would be of my work. Like faith itself, she brought light into my day.

I thought of Sister Peggy last week when I took on the job of editor. I understand that the engine of news and public debate means newspapers must often generate heat. I want our newspaper to also be a source of light.

Sister Peg might have ideas. I got too busy to call right away. Anyway, hundreds of readers had written, called and e-mailed with great suggestions.

I was going through a stack of this mail the other night when the phone rang. I heard that my 11-year-old son was having a severe asthma attack and was on his way to the emergency room. I raced to Horton Hospital.

I don't have to tell any parent what it feels like to see your child struggling for breath. Sam was taking his third intense nebulizer treatment as we waited for him to begin breathing easier. I absently put my hands in my pockets. Out came the envelope that was in my hand when I got the emergency phone call.

I opened it. It was a note wishing me "Mazel Tov" on my new job. It ended like this: "I keep you and your family in my prayers every day. Love, Sister Peggy."

I looked at my son. I showed him the outside of Sister Peggy's card, a photo of a radiant earth from outer space. Underneath was a quote from an astronaut. It said, "What I saw was just too beautiful to have happened by accident."

My son is feeling better. I lit my Sabbath candles with gratitude. Because light beams from people of different faiths, it must mean there are many paths to universal truth.

But religion is also very specific, beautiful in its details, its rituals, its radiant discoveries and celebrations.

That's why, with Christmas coming this week, I want to wish you more than the politically correct "Happy holidays." For all those who feel blessed by this sacred holiday, I wish you a Christmas of joy. I thank you for Sister Peggy Murphy and for everyone out there who, like faith itself, fills us with light.

Taking a Chance on Happiness

June 8, 1984

Within hours of meeting Lorraine Lee Lambach, I knew it was a match made in heaven.

She said she loves musical theater and performs in community productions. I like musical theater about as much as I enjoy going to the dentist.

I told her my idea of great Friday night is going to Yankee Stadium. She knew so much about baseball that she was certain Ron Guidry was a hockey player.

She's a mid-Hudson girl born and bred in rural Orange County. I'm a city boy, fresh from a life of subways.

To top it off, she appeared to be a happy woman who took the measure of people by their merits. I made my living by often getting cranky as a New Year's Day hangover.

With friends, I had all the room in the world for differences. In romances, I tended to take up with people who like the same things I do.

And this woman didn't fit in.

So why was I having such a good time?

***

It is 1966. I am 14 years old and have just broken up with the redhead from Nagle Avenue because she hates the Beatles. My mother is sitting across the dinner table and is not amused.

"Now, that's silly," she says. "There's more to love than just superficial things you have in common. Love is respecting differences. It's kindness, not criticism."

The lecture is over. I nod glumly and go on with my dinner. I figure my mom just hates the Beatles too.

It is a summer night of the same year. My father suggests we take a walk around the block. The night before, I had come home very late from a neighborhood dance. Dizzy with perfume and dusted with leaves from the park.

During the walk, my father starts a rambling discussion about the birds and bees. I give him a smirk, like I'm hip to all there is a fella needs to know on the subject.

"There's more to it than that," my father says, his voice catching in anger. "There is love. And don't ever forget this — there is respect. A woman must be a friend."

It is a winter night later in life. My father is on the telephone. It is a rare conversation between father and son. We are talking about love. I tell him of my disappointments.

"Mike, my boy," he says. "A lot of men fall for unhappy women. It makes them feel needed. The White Knight to the rescue — it's pure ego. But a man knows he is happy with himself when he falls in love with a happy woman."

We lift the weight of the conversation by ending it with some Rodney Dangerfield jokes. I get off the phone thinking there is love in our laughter.

***

I went to musicals and watched her perform. I couldn't take my eyes off her for a minute. If someone in the audience so much as coughed, I thought of murder.

She went with me to Yankee Stadium. She didn't even get up for popcorn because she said she didn't want to miss Ron Guidry scoring a goal.

There came a kindness, an ease, an electricity about our time together. We could make each other laugh whenever we wanted to.

It took a long time to realize my parents are pretty smart about this sort of thing. Smart enough to tell me that with everything they know about love, they are still awed by its mystery.

A parent's voice never really leaves the child. Some voices you listen to. Some you don't. I finally listened to my parents' voices about love. And I gave this mystery with the musical, happy, country girl a chance.

I'm glad I did.

Tomorrow, I'm going to marry the loveliest woman in the world. I have never been so happy in all my life.

Deep Down, Snow Is Child's Play

January 11, 1984

Global war could have been declared yesterday but it wouldn't have been Topic A of mid-Hudson conversation.

All day long, the talk in the offices, diners and factories sounded like the mid-Hudson was breathlessly awaiting the arrival of a fearsome miniature Martian.

"People tell me it's going to be a couple of feet," says Margaret Washington, the Town of Thompson clerk.

"I hear everything from 4 to 6 inches to 8 to 12," says Bob Lapidus, owner of Ettie's Deli in Newburgh. "And it might not come at all if it stays east."

"It's very confusing," says George Schnell, chairman of the state University College at New Paltz Geography Department. "I've heard as much as 8."

Aargh! Look up in the sky. It's a bird. It's a plane. It's snow.

Grown-ups feel required to put on solemn faces about such a subject as a major snowstorm.

It's like being a kid and watching the school principal slip on a lunchroom banana peel. "Isn't that awful, young John?" asks your teacher. "Oh yes, Miss Diddy," you say, trying to bite the smile off your lips.

We talk about the inconvenience. Lost income. Kids home from school. Danger.

But who's kidding whom? There's a part of us that thinks a snowstorm is great fun. No matter how deep we furrow our brow about snow, there's usually at least a dash of childish glee lurking right behind it.

Take the case of deli-master Lapidus. "Of course it hurts business," he says with all the good cheer of a sour pickle. "I have a nice catering job for 9 in the morning and I have to tell them I can't promise anything."

Yeah, but Bob, is there any part of you that's looking forward to a snowstorm?

All of a sudden, Lapidus takes on the naughty tone a kid contemplating hooky. "To tell you the truth, I'd love to take a day off," he says. "I think in a way, we all look forward to snow."

One Middletown guy who makes his living doing very responsible things admitted (only with the promise of anonymity) that he "couldn't wait" for the storm to hit. "Driving in a snowstorm is like having an illicit affair," he said. "You know it's dangerous as hell but there's something beautiful about it."

You don't get poetry like this about a partly cloudy day.

And you don't get a day off about it, either. Excitement about snow must begin as children when school closes if enough of it falls. We associate snow with the coziness of hot chocolate and momma pinning our mittens to our jackets. And, for a kid, snow makes the whole world seem like an amusement park.

With those pleasant associations in mind, it's hard to grow up and despise snow completely. Not even a serious snow-related injury five years ago has made Mrs. Washington of Monticello a real snow-hater. "Let me put it this way," she says. "I don't like the icy roads. But the major snowstorms are less dangerous in a way I don't mind them as much."

Granted, the thrill over snow will wear a little thin by the middle of February. It might even fade by this morning if you're out there trying to clear your driveway.

And to people who really have to suffer the effects of a storm, there's not a lick of fun about it. Listen, I'm worried myself. My '74 Chevy handles the ice and snow about as well as the Titanic.

But we have to admit, snow is heaven's most magnificent special effect. There's a wonder to it that makes us all children again.

So how 'bout it? On your mark, get set...Last one to build a snowman is a rotten egg.

Making Money vs. Making Your Mark

March 26, 2000

In this great gold rush, when a millionaire is born each minute, here is a story about making your mark. Ed Lloyd was here. Surely you remember the name. He was a local hero, a merchant pioneer, the emperor of the Main Street exodus.

Time was when everyone knew Lloyd's Super Center. When the Middletown merchant first built his mammoth store in rural Wallkill, they laughed at him. A supermarket and a department store all in one. In the middle of nowhere. Ha.

Legend has it that Ed Lloyd said he would live to see the grass grow on Main Street. He was just about right. While downtowns emptied, he built a kingdom of three hugely successful supercenters across Orange County.

You can't have forgotten Lloyd's, a place as groundbreaking as amazon.com. First grocery store in New York to have a self-service meat section. First to have its own pharmacy.

Ed Lloyd himself lived in a house on a hill overlooking his store. He was a nice man, often swallowed by loneliness and depression. He used to let neighborhood kids feed the fish in his backyard pond.

Sitting in his sprawling empty ranch, looking out on his empire, he once told me he wondered if he had made any lasting mark.

In a search for meaning, he took out newspaper ads dispensing advice about life. Rambling homilies about the tide of change, about politics, about foreign affairs. "Ed Lloyd says..." they began.

His often unpopular opinions were tolerated because we are taught to see financial success as a symbol of divine wisdom and worth.

But, in time, folks decided to buy their toothpaste at the global Wal-Mart. They called Ed Lloyd a dinosaur, a relic of the local age. He died in 1996 as his bankrupt business went belly-up.

Since then, his supercenter has collected cobwebs. The gold rush is up the road in the megamalls, on the fast lane of the internet shopping highway. The newly rich whiz by, confident and single-minded, certain of their mark.

This week, it was announced that wreckers will hack away at the old Lloyd's building on Route 211. A shining new Stop & Shop will replace it.

Ed Lloyd's mark of success is buried as if it never existed. Fewer and fewer people will remember his wealth or his store or the cutting edge of his success.

I asked my youngest son if he remembers anything about someone named Ed Lloyd.

Oh yes, he said. He was the man who let kids feed the fish in his pond.

It's something to think about in the swagger of this gold rush. Which leaves a more lasting impression, the getting or the giving? The financial killing or the small, kind gesture?

The gold rush beckons us to stake our time in the pursuit of wealth. The story of Ed Lloyd says be forewarned. Fortunes come, fortunes go. Businesses, boats, BMWs are swept away like children's toys caught in a stream.

All the while, in the still water of everyday life, we have opportunities to make a lasting ripple.

It Takes a Big Heart to Hear Cry of Despair

October 8, 2000

The day was heaving toward high noon. Still air hung over Conklin Lane in Harriman, cut only by the buzz of bees and the swarm of cars. Carol Coutant reached for the ringing phone.

A man's voice on the other end said, "I just want to talk to you before I die."

Who is this, she asked?

"I took my pills. I just want to say goodbye to you."

Who are you looking for?

"I'm sorry for everything."

His voice was slow, slurry. He said he had e-mailed her a lot. Carol Coutant knew the man had the wrong number.

She did not hang up. A life had fallen into her hands. She pretended she knew him.

"Who is this? Ted?"

No, said the man, "It's Tim."

"Tim, what are you doing?"

The diabetes, he said. He was 40 years old, and arthritis had nearly crippled him. The sleep disorder had turned his life into hell. All his ills had sent his true love packing. "I just can't take it any more."

He had swallowed enough barbiturates to kill himself. Carol kept talking with him, trying to find out where he was. His voice became halting and more slurred, and she had to listen harder to hear what he was saying. He was falling asleep, maybe forever.

"Tim," she said, desperate to locate him. "Did you get my letter?'"

No.

"Gee, I sent it where you told me. What's your address again, Tim?"

He gave it to her in mumbles. A town near Rocky Mount, N.C.

No street address, only a post-office box.

I'm no expert, she thought. I need help.

Carol Coutant clutched the cordless phone in her hand and began walking down the street toward the Harriman police station. The connection held.

She was upset. She told Officer Ray Culver what was going on. He started calling around to different police departments in the Rocky Mount area. The postmaster got the man's address in North Carolina.

The Harriman police called down to the sheriff's department there. They got hold of the postmaster and found the address.

Paramedics rushed for his house.

Carol went back home, held the fading man on the line, calling him back to life. She heard pounding.

"Tim, there's someone there for you. Open up your door. Get up."

He couldn't move. Carol talked to the paramedics on a separate cell phone. Ma'am, do you mind if we break open the door?

"I'm in New York. I don't know the man. I can't...Yes, go ahead."

The next sound she heard was the crush of paramedics. The man was rushed to the hospital. Doctors began pumping his stomach as he lay moments from death.

***

Carol Coutant says she was unprepared for this encounter. But where we go in these moments is where we came from. Coutant is from an old farm family in Monroe.

Dig under the K-Mart there on Route 17M, and you will find their soil.

When her grandparents would hear of trouble in town, they'd fill a wagon with food and have Carol roll it to the house in need. It could be a death in the family, an illness, a lonely soul. She learned you do not turn a deaf ear to sorrow.

Generations later, a prison guard from North Carolina on his way to death pushes buttons on a telephone and reaches her.

The cry of the lonely is always ringing somewhere — in our town, our workplace, maybe even in our own homes. Who will hear it?

Carol Coutant listened so well, a man from Rocky Mount, N.C., just drove all the way to Harriman to thank her for saving his life.

Jake's October Run Still Rises in the Dust

October 22, 2000

God, Jake could play. They can still see his spikes digging in the dairyland mud.

They can hear his bat crack a line drive toward the cow field and his beefsteak legs pound for first. Watch Jake churn past second, then bull-snort around third as racing outfielders chase a baseball deep into the loins of April.

If you lived in this patch of the Hudson Valley in 1973, you weren't surprised that Karl "Jake" Jacobsen left town as a top pick of the Kansas City Royals. You were surprised he came home so soon.

You saw Jake in a bar muttering about bad breaks, idiot managers, coach's favorites.

Jake kept talking about it long after people stopped listening. This is farm country, where disappointment is part of the soil. Folks said Jake would have to look failure and unfairness in the eye and get on with life.

He shot heroin instead. Jake hit on his friends for money until he had none of either. He stole from his family. He fathered a child with another drug addict, then deserted them both. He bounced in and out of jail.

Until one day, 20 years later, Jake found himself fed up with the sound of his junkie lies. He owned up to the failure of his baseball career. He saw that when the better curve balls began to dance under his bat, he had tanked his pain with booze. He'd stayed down like a chump with a chip on his shoulder.

Now seeing what he had to do, Jake got sober. He found a job fixing roofs. He reclaimed his daughter, raising her himself. He made amends with friends and peace with family.

He walked past failure.

One afternoon, Jake was working on a roof when he got dizzy. No work, no pay, so he kept going. Sweat dripped and fever raged.

Turned out Jake had Lou Gehrig's disease. It ran through him something terrible. Soon, his muscles withered and his feet wobbled. By autumn, his speech had slurred horribly. He walked on rubber legs.

Jake kept raising his daughter, though. One October weekend during the baseball playoffs, she had a sleepover. In the morning, Jake took the kids to a ballfield in Pine Bush. He had the kids race around the bases in opposite directions. Whoever gets back to home plate first wins. He watched the children fly.

That's when Jake got it in his head to bolt for first. Lifting his worn legs, crippled Karl Jacobsen kept pumping until he began to run. Go, Jake, go.

Almost to the base, Jake fell in a heap. Seeing her father slumped on the base paths, his daughter began to cry. Jake started to laugh.

"Don't worry," he said. "Daddy's been down before. I'll get up."

Legs flopping, arms noodly, Jake tried to rise. He had stumbled into the glorious season of the World Series.

Now we recall Larsen's day, Reggie's night, Clemente's week. But picture, too, a dying Karl Jacobsen chugging to first, crumbling in the dirt as dead leaves swirled, then trying to plant his feet so his daughter could see him stand.

Jake finally made it upright on scarecrow pins, laughing until she laughed, too.

Holding the championship banner of the flawed and the doomed, Karl Jacobsen walked into winter head held high. What was left of his body soon turned to ashes. The remains of his October run rise in the dust of every late-inning rally.

Adam Finds the Light

December 19, 2000

Mike Levine wrote this Hudson Valley fable a few years ago for children trying to find meaning in their holiday amidst the glitz of Christmas. As Hanukkah approaches, we want to share this story with you again.

I'm 12 years old and I never understood Hanukkah. My parents would kill me for saying this but it seemed like a Christmas booby prize for Jewish kids. Boy, I'm in trouble now.

I mean the Hanukkah story happened about a million years ago.

Everyone had a beard back then, I think, even the kids. What's the point? My Christian friends, they got all these cool movies about Christmas.

And Christmas trees and lights, wow. I used to wish I had all that. Until yesterday.

It all started a few hours before the first night of Hanukkah. I won't lie.

We were jumping crazy on the school bus.

Crystal and Kevin sang "Jingle Bells, Batman Smells." Keeshawn shouted his lines from the school Christmas play. I played the drums on Eddie's back while Carlos rapped: "From Highland Falls to Greenwood Lake, school is out for Christmas break!"

Almost every house on the ride home was lit up with green and red bulbs. It looked really cool. Then we passed my house.

Crystal said, "Yo, Adam, where are your Christmas lights?'" Everyone stared at me. I turned red. "We don't have any," I mumbled. "We're Jewish."

Kevin, said, oh, yeah, you celebrate Hanukkah or something. The other kids looked at me, not mean or anything. Just kind of like they felt sorry.

You don't even get a Christmas tree? asked Luis. No. I tried to change the subject. So what's everyone doing over vacation? Turns out all my friends were doing Christmas stuff — Christmas karoake at the mall, Christmas parties at each other's house, going to Christmas shows, Christmas everything.

"Wanna help me decorate our tree?" asked Carlos. I don't know, I said, as we landed at my bus stop. Anyone want to play ball? Yeah, maybe, they said.

"Merry Christmas," said the bus driver as I jumped out at the corner.

I began to walk home. Looking at all the Christmas lights, I felt lonesome. I always did this time of year.

When I was 5, I couldn't figure out why Santa skipped our house. I thought I was a bad boy. Or maybe Santa hated Jewish kids.

My parents said Santa belonged to another holiday. But why couldn't we at least have Christmas lights and a tree? We'd still be Jewish, right?

Mom, I said as I opened the front door, don't you think Christmas lights look cool? Oh, they're very pretty, she said. She stood in the living room dusting off the menorah. She was standing on a perfect spot for a Christmas tree.

My father was in the kitchen peeling potatoes for Hanukkah latkes. He whistled a song about dreidels. They were both in a good mood.

So, I said, "I have a great idea. Let's have our own Christmas lights. And our own Christmas tree." Absolutely not, my mom said.

Aw, how come, what's the big deal? My dad stopped peeling potatoes. He stopped whistling, too. He looked me in the eye and spoke slow and serious.

"Adam, Christmas is a wonderful Christian holiday. It's for Christians." I didn't get it. As far as I could see, Christmas seemed to be about lights and Santa. So we can't have a Christmas tree? I asked again.

No, said my mother, starting to get mad. "We light a menorah for Hanukkah. It's beautiful." I don't really get Hanukkah.

I heard the story a hundred times. The Jews wouldn't bow down to statues so they battled with their foreign rulers. A tiny ragtag band called the Maccabees re-captured the temple.

They only had enough oil to light the temple for one night. But it lasted eight days. That's the whole shebang.

So how come I can't have a Christmas tree, I asked.

Because when you really understand Hanukkah, said my mom, you won't want a Christmas tree.

This was a losing battle. I was angry, too, tired of being left out. "Why can't we celebrate Christmas like everyone else? Would it kill us?" It might, said my dad.

I said I was going over to Carlos' house. As I closed the door, I heard them say be back by nightfall so we can light the menorah. I still wanted Christmas lights.

I walked down the street checking out all the Christmas lights. Hey, Carlos, I said knocking on his door, wanna play ball? His father called out to him to be back by nightfall.

By the time we walked down to the clearing in the park, we had recruited Keeshawn, Crystal, Kevin, Nestor and his kid brother who had a football.

Big problem. A bunch of high schoolers had taken over the field. They were drinking beer.

I looked at Carlos. Hey, guys, I said, if you're not playing, can we have the field? I was shaking as I said it.

Two guys as big as oak trees came up to me and Carlos. Sure, kid, let's see you drink a beer first. Carlos and I shook our heads no.

What about you, said five more guys circling around Keeshawn and Crystal. Have a beer. Let's see if you're big enough to play. It'll be cool.

No, said Crystal, her knees trembling. No, said Keeshawn, we don't do that. That's not who we are.

Then this really mean guy we knew as Rockhead stood over Nestor's kid brother. Hey, pipsqueak, said Rockhead, I'll give you a beer for that football. With that, he took our football and squirted beer all over us.

We ran like crazy to our secret hiding place over behind Black Rock.

Nestor's brother was crying. I was scared, too.

What are we going to do, we asked each other. Nestor said maybe we should take a sip just to get the field. No way, the rest of us said, we're not drinking any stupid beer.

That's when I had an idea. You know that swamp across the road — the one that looks fine until you step in it and then you get mud up to your knees? We hatched our plan and ran down to the field with the big kids.

"See you suckers," Carlos told them. "We're going to a better field than this. It's our secret place. It has benches, too." Yeah, I said, there's even beer buried there.

They fell for it. Rockhead grabbed Keeshawn and said you better tell us where it is. He gave them directions to the swamp. They all left.

When they were a block away, we fell down laughing. Those bullies were going to get a mud bath and we had our field back.

It was getting dark already. Kevin ran home and got four lantern flashlights. I don't think they'll work, he said, the batteries are dead.

But guess what? The lanterns worked. It was like some sort of miracle.

We played until we heard the muddy bullies shouting at us.

We all ran home. "Mom, Dad," I said, catching my breath. "You'll never guess what happened." I told them the whole story.

My father broke out into a big grin. Boy, he was beaming. I had never seen him so excited.

"You did it!" he said. "That's the story of Hanukkah! You lived it." What? And then it hit me. Yessss.

These bullies were like the evil rulers in the second century. They wanted us to knuckle under. My friends and I were like the Maccabees.

We stood up for who we were.

Getting our field back was like getting the temple back. "And Kevin's lanterns with the dead batteries, that was like the miracle of the lights." My mother kissed me. I even let her.

"Hanukkah is about being who you are," she said. "It was the first time ever a people fought against bullies for the freedom to pray their own way — to be themselves. Now you're part of the Hanukkah story."

Everything clicked. I still thought Christmas was beautiful, but it wasn't fair to celebrate someone else's holiday. Especially when we had our own.

There was something magical about that first night of Hanukkah. The menorah sparkled. Carlos stopped over to our house. He ate latkes and I showed him how to spin a dreidel.

Then I went over to his house. His parents served this really cool Mexican holiday custard. They sang Christmas carols in Spanish.

By the time I started walking back, it was dark and snowing. The only light was the warm glow from the holiday displays. Some lights shone for Christmas, some for Kwanzaa.

And when I saw the window with the Hanukkah menorah burning bright, I knew I was home.

A Sacred, Special Morning

I wrote this column a decade ago. Since then, many parents have told me it's a way they mark the arrival of September's first school bus. I've added a few lines for today. Here's to a safe and healthy year for all our children.

Quick, before they leave this morning. Take a good look. Touch their faces, run your hands through their hair.

We got antsy with them last month, but now we want time to stand still. Like falling leaves and chilly mornings, some great force signals us today. We are aware of life passing.

See the kindergartner with a brave, bewildered smile watching her mother cry as the school bus pulls away. The high school freshman with a lump in his throat hears his father whisper everything will be OK. Brothers and sisters who fought all summer now hold hands.

Today is proud, today is helpless, today is tomorrow. This is a special morning, wrenching and sacred.

As a young reporter, I'd wonder why. What's the big deal about the first day of school? I would write down quotes in my notebook and comprehend nothing.

Then I became a parent. I found out. We mark time by today.

On this morning, we remember our own parents and our own childhood. We are filled with the smell of old raincoats, the sticky bond of classroom glue, the childhood knot of worried excitement. We were so small and lost. (Secret: A part of us is still lost. We tell no one.)

Now we have children of our own. On this morning, we remember the holy moment of their birth.

We see this is all just a matter of time. Once, we thought our children were ours alone. Each September, on this day, we learn better. Nothing is ours to keep.

Time passes through our eyes this morning. We see our children as newborns, we picture them as grown-ups. We see them walking their own children to school.

Time passes in the beat of a heart. I have seen my kindergarten boy walk into his dorm on his first day of college. Last year, I watched my younger son leave on a jet plane for a semester in Israel. I stood there, at once empty and full, as frightened and proud as the morning his first school bus pulled away.

Come on, it's getting late. The bus is coming up the road. I'll keep this short.

Make sure they have everything they need. Double check. Write their name on the book bag. Sweetheart, did you remember your lunch money? Dad, don't call me mushy stuff in front of the other kids.

They are right. Like the summer birds leaving us, our children know what to do. Like September leaves waving on the trees, we, too, give way to the winds of change.

A Little Girl's Grace Lives on at Thanksgiving

November 24, 2005

Once upon a Thanksgiving, 9-year-old Debbie Lynn Matoren saw a restaurant full of diners eating their holiday meals without a word of grace. The girl from Wallkill took out a crumpled piece of paper. With all the power her tiny voice could muster, she announced, "I would like to read this to you."

She chimed a grace she had read in this newspaper. The grumpy diners bowed their heads. The girl's grace helped them feel whole and blessed.

A few months later, Debbie was in school dancing for joy when her heart stopped beating. She was buried on a pale January morning in 1988. Her mom asked me for a copy of the Thanksgiving column Debbie had read.

Each Thanksgiving, to keep a young girl's memory alive, we publish this small community grace I wrote 20 years ago to celebrate the birth of my first child. Over the years, children and elders have offered additional blessings. You may wish to add yours for, once again, we gather as one community around the harvest table.

We bow our heads. We give thanks:

For the bounty before us, however modest.

For those who toiled in field and kitchen to bring us this meal.

For sun and rain, soil and seed, the faithful harvest.

For the company that shares our table; for the loved ones missing but still with us.

For all the generations who brought us to this day.

We can grumble if we like. We can focus on family squabbles, numb out on food and football, get crazy over traffic. Or we can praise our gifts:

Water at the turn of a faucet.

A roof between us and the cold night.

A walk in the meadow under sparkling heavens.

The healing power of a tender touch.

Our elders, whose heirloom is wisdom.

The children who give us a window to eternity.

Our daily bread.

We can worship the gods of getting and spending. We can mistake amusement for joy, complacency for peace, cynicism for truth. But today we are thankful for:

The cord connecting us to the needy.

The visit of conscience allowing us to right our wrongs.

The generous souls who give to the greater good.

Those who protect us from harm.

The whisper of peace in the world and in our own lives.

Do we live like the walking dead? Do we forget life's possibilities, our capacity for wonder? Not today. We stand in awe before:

The thunder and lightning of passion.

The private dream of words and music.

The cleansing sweep of laughter and tears.

The enduring comfort of friendship.

The unbreakable bonds of family love.

Forgiveness.

Days and years roll on, one to another, and we wonder, where did the time go? But when we know our blessings, each moment is eternal. And so we say grace for our miracles:

The four seasons teaching us to number our days.

Love that is stronger than death.

The promise of a new morning when the lonely are embraced, the sick healed, the tortured set free.

The sanctuary of memory.

The breath of our Creator, pulsing through this room and through all of us everywhere.

Strange how entitlement brings us emptiness, but gratitude fills our cup. Savor each breath and blessing. Remember the time you laughed so hard, jumped so high, held so tight. Remember the hour when you watched the scarlet sky fold to night. Remember the holy moment when you touched the tiny fingers of birth.

Thanks to all who have come before us for showing us the way. We see you in all we love. And to everyone under the bow of this grace, a sweet Thanksgiving.

Find the Possibility in 2007's New Days

After running the gauntlet of work and obligation and stress, the end of 2006 leaves many folks feeling nothing but weary. We stumble to a finish line only to get up and start a new race. Will 2007 be the same stuff, different year?

It doesn't have to be. Look back on the journey of 2006 and remember all the tiny gems and miracles of the year gone by. The small kindnesses, the welcoming hand, the unexpected laughter. Look back and we know not only what was, but what can be.

Today, we can feel it in our bones. It pounds in the heart. There's a new year coming and its name is possibility.

So may this be the year when you seize each day. The year when you start something big.

Go on, make a promise to yourself you can keep and light up a dream.

You'll need to travel lighter. Drop that baggage dragging you down. This will be the year when anger turns to forgiveness. When couples who once saw the best in each other see it again. When parents and children reunite. The grudge is over, for in case you haven't heard, life ends in a blink.

In the next life, our sages say, we will be called to account for all the good things on this earth we did not enjoy. May this be the year when a new song makes your heart race. When you get up and dance. When you rediscover passion in your work, your play, your partner.

Loosen up. Shake off old habits. Take a walk in new woods. This can be the year when we connect ourselves to something greater than ourselves. When we escape the prison of self and loosen the shackles of envy.

This will be the year when the age of polarity recedes. The looney tune of the conspiracist and the screed of the name caller will fade as their mean season has passed. Sing a song for civility. May we call on something better from ourselves and each other. When we live less as childlike consumers and more as citizens who give and engage.

May this be the year when we stop blaming others for our failings. When we hold our tongues from malice and open our mouths in praise. Praise for the seasons. Praise for life. Praise for our loved ones. Praise even for those who have done us wrong.

Most people are aching to do the right thing, the kind thing. We want to leave the world a better place. So may this be the year when we each do something to repair the damage, when we band together to see that no teen's life is snuffed out in a crash of twisted metal.

We know there will be storms and heartbreak. May we roll with the haymakers. This will be the year when we do not shrink away from our pain or the grief of the bereaved. For some in our Times Herald-Record family, this has been a year of crushing personal loss. May shattered hearts everywhere begin to heal. Weeping may tarry for the night, we are told, but joy cometh in the morning.

And for all who feel stuck, beaten down or stressed out in taken-for-granted situations, who feel ground down by toil or worry or loneliness: Hang in there.

This will be the year when the long shot comes roaring down the backstretch. When someone discovers the wonder of you. Come out of your shell, for the parade's about to begin.

Here's to 2007. A child will learn to read. Someone will fall in love for the first time. There will be weddings and celebrations. An elder will spin stories that connect the generations.

They know the night will pass. There will be light. There will be morning.

It is the first day of a new year called possibility.

Afterword

Mike left behind a small blue book entitled "Things I've Learned" that was found by his sons, Ben and Sam Levine, under the driver's seat of his Ford Focus the week after he died.

The book contained the candid thoughts Mike had in his quieter moments.

Here's some of them:

"When I'm in a coma, a prison, a stroke — I want to recall how unruly and passionate life is."

"In the end, the verdict isn't whether life has been good to us, but whether we've been good to life. What a gift. What a treasure to be aware of our mortality, of time ticking. This is not rhetoric. This is what gets me up in the morning."

"We all do our best, I think. We all miss the mark. We get points for getting up each day, trying hard, mostly being kind to each other, knowing what's coming in the end."

"I never take disagreement personally and I'm always surprised when people do. I come from NYC where people always went at it and then had a beer."

"I'm loathe to rehash my day — I had a hard enough time living it in the first place."

"What is it like to have your body betray you? We will all find out. The neurons misfire, the synapses don't click. The auto-immune response of dying of old age — depression, loss of hearing, unsteady legs. Sooner or later, life shows its claws. We all fail. There is a 100 percent mortality rate for our species. Jews never wear their tallis (prayer shawls) at night. But on Yom Kippur evening, we come to schul in our prayer shawls. Because we will be buried in them. And it reminds us to have a little rachmones (compassion) for each other. To see each other as mortals so we will not judge each other so severely."

"It's not the answers that matter — it's the questions."

"If I knew I was leaving my part of the world in worse shape, I couldn't shave in the morning."

"I went on for another hour or two at work, spreading the gospel of alternative story telling to a young reporter. What a privilege it is for me to have this job."

"My current job may feel frustrating at times, aggravating, alienating, foreign — but it always feels noble, as if I had suddenly been cast into the Resistance during WWII. To spark a flame, to mentor others, to fight against the tide of history crushing not only newspapers, but thoughtfulness. To protect jobs, to make peace where there is strife, to challenge, to do the decent thing when no one is around to give you applause but you have the faint hope humankind will benefit — that's all worthy."

"May I have the guts to feel it all."

"You want to find out why you're as screwed up as the next person, knock yourself out. But don't let it paralyze you. You might want to just accept who you are and go out living. There's health and neurosis in all of us. I don't know — I think I must be shallow or too much of a sensualist but I like to dive headfirst. So sometimes you come up with a pile of shit on your face. Big deal."

"Telling people's stories was a way of finding out about my own. It was one of the few ways I could feel some transcendent force of life some people call God. I hope I get to do it again."

"I load up each day with genuine hope and I don't come home until I'm shot."

"We all have worth beyond our economic usefulness. Who says so? That's when I call on a God with no name and no face and no promise of heaven. Who is rooting for us. Who is One with all we are. Who is as complex as Life, Who respects the laws of nature and science and Who has left us all with a spark of the divine. And that spark connects us one to the other, compels us to repair the world, to join the sparks so it becomes an eternal light."

"I find that I'm stronger than I could ever have imagined. I'm no hero — I just follow some sort of compass someone has thankfully instilled inside me."

"I can't give in to the sin of despair. Despair is considered a sin because it is an approach to life...the Talmud says that in the next life, we will be called to account for all the good things on earth we did not enjoy. Despair works against that."

"I am glad to be alive to feel all of this. Life is grand."

About the Author

Mike Levine was the editor of *Heights-Inwood*, a weekly newspaper in Manhattan, before he began working as a reporter at the *Times Herald-Record* in Middletown, N.Y., in 1980.

In 1983, he convinced the editor to give him a try as a columnist. Levine felt he had found his calling and readers thought so too.

His stories celebrating the spirit of everyday people earned state and national awards, with some featured in *Reader's Digest*. Levine served as the newspaper's writing coach and city editor before becoming executive editor in 1999.

As most of Levine's brilliance occurred inside his head, he was known for his inability to manage himself in the physical world. With the patient help of his assistant, Taryn Clark, Levine made a passable imitation of being semi-organized.

But by the end of the day – despite her best efforts – his tie was askew, his shoes were untied, his shirttail was hanging out, and his reading glasses (one of five he bought from the drugstore) were horribly smudged.

His personal appearances notwithstanding, Levine was a precise and relentless practitioner when it came to language. In his writing and his editing, choosing the right word was his obsession and finding the perfect arc of the story was his aim.

He left the *Times Herald-Record* in 2001 to join *ESPN the Magazine* in New York City as a senior editor. His work there contributed to the magazine's 2002 award for General Excellence by the American Society of Magazine Editors.

He returned to the *Times Herald-Record* as executive editor in 2002, and led the newspaper to numerous awards. It was his leadership that caused CNN's Aaron Brown to hold it up one morning and declare it "this feisty little newspaper in upstate New York!"

Levine gave all he had to the *Times Herald-Record*, and died suddenly at age 54, in 2007, when his heart gave out.

Upon Levine's death, Pete Hamill, the author, columnist and former editor of the *New York Post*, said: "Mike was one of the best newspapermen I ever knew, full of passion for our poor imperfect craft."

About the Editor

Christopher Mele is a veteran newsman who, growing up in the Bronx, knew at the age of 11 that he wanted to cover the news. He graduated from New York University with a degree in journalism and worked in the Adirondack Mountains of New York at the *Adirondack Daily Enterprise* in Saranac Lake and the (Plattsburgh) *Press-Republican* before joining the *Times Herald-Record* in Middletown, N.Y., in 1992. At the *Times Herald-Record*, Mele was an investigative reporter and editor and a regional, Sunday and training editor who worked with Mike Levine on a number of projects. Mele was named executive editor of the *Pocono Record* in Stroudsburg, Pa., in 2009. He joined the Metro copy desk of *The New York Times* in 2014, and is currently a senior staff editor and weekend editor of the Express Team at the *Times*.

About Team Mike

Members of "Team Mike," the group that served as the sounding board and pillars of support in helping see this project through to completion, include Mike's widow, Ellen Levine, and three journalists who worked with Levine in his newsroom at the *Times Herald-Record*: his managing editor, Meg McGuire; reporter and columnist, Steve Israel; and editor and senior manager, Barbara Gref.

About
the Publisher

The Sager Group was founded in 1984. In 2012 it was chartered as a multimedia content brand, with the intent of empowering those who create art — an umbrella beneath which makers can pursue, and profit from, their craft directly, without gatekeepers. TSG publishes books; ministers to artists and provides modest grants; designs logos, products and packaging, and produces documentary, feature, and commercial films. By harnessing the means of production, The Sager Group helps artists help themselves. To read more from The Sager Group, visit www.TheSagerGroup.net

More Books

By The Sager Group

The Stories We Tell: Classic True Tales by America's Greatest Women Journalists

New Stories We Tell: True Tales by America's Next Generation of Great Women Journalists

Newswomen: Twenty-five Years of Front Page Journalism

Next Wave: America's New Generation of Great Literary Journalists

Artful Journalism: Essays in the Craft and Magic of True Storytelling

Everybody Leaves Behind a Name: True Stories by Michael Brick

Artifex Te Adiuva

Made in the USA
Middletown, DE
19 May 2019